Truancy and School Phobias

In London alone well over 6,000 pupils play truant from school every day, and throughout the country the continuing rise in truancy rates among teenagers worries parents, teachers and local authorities.

The discovery that a child has not been going to school after leaving home "normally" in the morning, but has been wandering about on his own without food or supervision all day, can come as a great shock to parents. Also, the deep-seated apprehensions of the children who go absent need understanding.

In this timely book Mr. Denney describes some causes of truancy and school phobias and the ways in which educationalists are trying to help; he also examines how relationships within the family affect the way a child reacts to the experience of "education" in the total sense of the word, and assesses the completely new approach now being developed towards the social and psychiatric services available to school-children and their parents.

Parental awareness of the child's problems and needs is vital if a solution is to be found. It is to encourage such awareness that this book has been added to the Care and Welfare Library.

PRIORY EDITORIAL CONSULTANTS

THE CARE AND WELFARE LIBRARY
Consultant Medical Editor: Alexander R. K. Mitchell
MB, ch.B, MRCPE, MRCPsych

Truancy and School Phobias

The Rev. A. H. Denney

AKC, BA
Diocesan Director of Education, Coventry

PRIORY PRESS LIMITED

The Care and Welfare Library

SBN 85078 164 7
Copyright © 1973 by The Rev. A. H. Denney
First published in 1974 by
Priory Press Limited
101 Grays Inn Road London WC1
Made and printed in Great Britain by
The Garden City Press Limited
Letchworth, Hertfordshire SG6 1JS

Contents

Foreword

IN the last year attention has been drawn by press and television to the increasing number of children who, for one reason or another, are failing to attend school regularly. A high proportion of these children are described as "truants." The word is a familiar one and most of us have a fair idea of what truancy is. Many of us no doubt played truant when we were young and find it hard to take the matter very seriously. But when we look closer we find that many of the "truants" are unhappy, lonely children, quite unlike our memory of ourselves for whom it was a "lark" which was usually met with some punishment for which we were quite prepared. Those who investigate the backgrounds and lives of the modern truant have cause for considerable anxiety; the parents of truanting children have reason to suspect that something more than mischievousness is at stake. Truancy is becoming recognized as an emotional disturbance which may go deep into the personal life and growth of the child, a reaction to circumstances over which he has no control, a way of behaving to which he is driven rather than one which he chooses.

School-phobia, about which there is a growing volume of study and literature, is much more dramatic in its observable effects. A child may wish to attend school with his friends, seem to have nothing amiss with himself when he is at school, yet be quite incapable of making the journey from home to school without the expression of great anxiety and misery which deeply affects both

7

himself and his parents. Such children may be a very small minority of those attending school, but no parent or teacher who has witnessed their very obvious distress can fail to want to help them out of such misery.

This book is written mainly for parents but also for any who are concerned with the well-being of children and would like to understand a little of what lies behind their behaviour and what may be done to help them back to normality.

The experiences of teachers and social workers and the help and advice of professionally concerned members of the educational services have all been used in many different ways and the contributions of children themselves have added greatly to the author's feeling of being close to what it really feels like to be unable to go to school.

I am most grateful to all those whose advice I have sought and who have answered questions so patiently. My particular thanks to "Valerie" whose account of herself is given at some length in Chapter 3.

A. H. Denney

I

The Results of Research

RESEARCH in any area of human behaviour has certain difficulties which not every researcher can overcome. In the first place we are dealing with human beings who cannot be submitted to scientific investigation with the same degree of objectivity and certainty which is possible with the rest of the natural order. No two children are precisely the same, and none will react in precisely the same way as his fellows to the same treatment or stimulus, so far as his emotional life and behaviour are concerned. No two children, even within the same family, have exactly the same upbringing or are subject to precisely the same pressures and influences.

Parents treat their own children differently, in spite of all efforts to be fair and impartial. Some children are jealous of their brothers and sisters, others show no such characteristics. Even in the most devoted families there are favouritisms which affect relationships, and every family case-worker is only too aware of the dangers of generalizing about the dynamics of the family group; every case is a wholly new and different case.

The circumstances in which children grow up are also very different for each individual child. Even children who live next door to one another will relate differently to the physical circumstances of their homes and their street; the interior of each home is shaped by the personalities of the parents and these differ from one another in a multiplicity of ways. We are used to making broad classifications of people and their neighbourhoods such

9

as "working class," "middle class," "council estate," "high rise flats" or "private development." But such terms only express a very vague pattern of type and life style, and tell us nothing of the real people who inhabit these places.

One could go on indefinitely stressing the factors which make people different from one another. But it is essential, however obvious it may seem, to understand how difficult it makes research into the causes and treatment of human behaviour. To this truancy and school-phobia are no exceptions. Both are forms of behaviour which appear to be departures from normality, but even this raises the questions of what is "normal" and is there such a creature as a "normal" child. No doubt, at one time or another, every parent has asked this question about his own children. Likewise, every parent has marvelled at the difference between each child in his own family.

All these differences have to be taken into account by the researcher who is looking for ways of measuring and assessing a particular type of behaviour. He describes them as "variables" in the situation he is examining, and he devises methods of taking them into account when making his assessments. He will decide what the variables are, or at least what seem to be the important ones. He will then group together those children with the same variable, for example, age, I.Q., type of school and so on, so that each group is as much alike in its composition as possible. He can study that group and make certain statements about the ways in which those children behave, and so associate a particular type of behaviour with a group having particular common characteristics. Similarly he can take a sample of, say, forty children who at one time or another have been persistent truants. He can then apply the variables as a means of grouping them, and see how many fall into each group.

For example, he may find that the age at which most children played truant was the common age for transfer from one school to another; or he may find that truants come predominantly from homes in which parental care is minimal (a factor which will need to be defined); or he may find that they come from schools which exercise a particular type of discipline. This is, of course, where the size and variety of the sample become very important. The smaller the sample the greater is the danger of unknown variables interfering with the accuracy of the assessment. For example, a small group of children may show a characteristic which is associated with local circumstances, or events which are of a temporary nature. The larger and more widely spread the sample, the more chance of small variables being discounted and the more general characteristics emerging.

In view of all these factors it is not surprising that research into child behaviour frequently comes up with almost as many answers as there are researchers in the field. When looking at the statistics and research which has been done into truancy and school-phobia these things must be kept in mind, it is unwise to accept uncritically any one group of findings. As far as possible it is necessary to look at the whole area of research and try to separate out what seem to be the general conclusions. In this particular field we still have a long way to go before we reach any certainty. But the work so far done helps our understanding of the seemingly meaningless behaviour of some children, and will give us greater confidence in our efforts to help them.

Research so far

If the general reader examines the library shelves for studies of truancy or school-phobia he will probably only find three books which deal specifically with the two problems, but much of what we know is summarized by their authors: Kahn and Nursten in *Unwillingly to School*, Tyerman in *Truancy* and Clyne in *Absent*. Yet, as the long lists of studies given in both Kahn and Clyne show, the total literature is quite considerable. Much is repetitive, in that past evidence is drawn upon to compare with or support the findings of a further piece of research. Almost all the literature relates truancy in one way or another to inadequacies in the home background. But the actual content of this "inadequacy" is not always made clear. A further difficulty lies in the reluctance of researchers to define truancy and school-phobia for the reasons already discussed, viz. the difficulty of separating the two categories of school refusal with any real degree of exactitude. The only difference that emerges with any real certainty is that truancy is a social rather than an emotional problem, associated with poor housing conditions and inadequate home care; while school-phobia is associated with a higher class background and seems to be emotional rather than social.

Three writers have drawn attention to the social factors in truancy. Of these Tyerman is the most recent, and the findings of his study are worth examining. He took a group of forty truants and subdivided this group into those who were persistent truants without the knowledge of their parents; those who were truants although their parents knew of it; those who were occasional truants without parental knowledge, and those who were occasional truants in spite of parental knowledge. The first interesting fact that emerges is that only two of the forty were girls, and these were occasional not persistent truants. This is a general finding among writers on truancy, and is a distinction that can reasonably be drawn between truancy and school-phobia.

When examining the relationship between truancy and home circumstances, Tyerman found very definite correlations between poor home circumstances and persistent truancy without the knowledge of parents. He singles out a number of factors relating to home background which are closely associated with truancy. Among these are the poor physical conditions of the home, the relationships between children and parents, the use of corporal punishment in the home, lack of parental interest in the child's welfare and the lack of strong ties with a responsible adult of good standards. Another writer, L. A. Hersou, studied fifty children who had been truant for periods of more than two months. He confirmed much of Tyerman's findings but added other factors which Tyerman did not assess. He found that twenty-three of his sample of fifty came from homes in which the mother was absent for prolonged periods during the first five years of the child's life, and twenty-four from homes in which the father was absent. These figures seem to imply an association between truancy and the one-parent family, but because one-parent families give rise to many stresses for both children and parent, it is difficult to isolate specific results and associate them with this single cause. Tyerman refers to unclean homes, inadequate clothing and lack of parental interest; these are all consequences of the single-parent situation and therefore the truancy could be caused by these factors rather than the absence of the parent. It is almost impossible, with the small samples provided by these writers, to make direct associations between truancy and the variables which are recorded.

Tyerman also draws attention to the low I.Q. which prevails among his sample, two-thirds of the group falling between 74 and 102. Perhaps more significant, but in line with what was recorded about home background, is the fact that three-quarters of the sample lacked affection, a third had been charged with stealing—a common reaction to the lack of affection—and a quarter had slept out or run away from home. Tyerman concludes:

The correlations suggest that certain circumstances are of particular importance. Among the most obvious is

the truant's failure at school, in his work, in his relations with other pupils, and often also, with his
teachers. Along with unhappiness at school there is
often unhappiness at home. Many are lonely and
miserable.

This conclusion suggests that truants are generally
suffering from a considerable degree of personal maladjustment. Indeed, Hersou's sample was drawn from
children whose emotional disturbance was sufficient for
them to have been referred to the Children's Department
of the Maudesley Hospital.

Another writer who comments on the emotional condition of truants is Dr. D. H. Stott, well known for his
studies of unsettled and delinquent children. Unlike the
writers referred to above, he secured a large national
sample of truants. One hundred and sixty-eight welfare
officers sent him, in all, 305 children representing their
two most recent truants, one from primary school and
the other from secondary school. Although some could
not supply both, the sample was both larger and more
widely spread nationally than most researchers had used.
His assessments of the truants were made in accordance
with the Bristol Social Adjustment Guide, a very detailed
analysis of the emotional conditions of children for which
Dr. Stott himself was responsible, and which is widely
used to assess social and emotional adjustment in children.
The Guide was filled in either by the child's class teacher
or from the reports of the welfare officers.

Dr. Stott found a high level of maladjustment among
the truants, both girls and boys. Unfortunately the definition of a truant may vary very considerably from one
welfare officer to another, and the inclusion in the sample
of cases of school-phobia, as well as of conventional truancy, is very probable and no distinction is drawn between the two. This research does, however, establish

even more firmly the fact that truancy is not just a problem of wilful indiscipline, but one of real maladjustment
demanding treatment at a clinic or hospital.

The fact of prevailing maladjustment or personal inadequacy should not entirely blind us to the existence of
a form of truancy which is a social norm for the group
from which the truant comes. Anti-authoritarianism for
varying reasons, prevails among some social groups, of
which gypsies are an example. School attendance is looked
upon as a departure from the normal behaviour pattern
of the group and is flouted because it is not seriously regarded as either necessary or desirable. This attitude may
not indicate any personal maladjustment or inadequacy,
but simply reflects the mores of a particular subculture.
To treat such children as maladjusted would be both unfair and fruitless.

Truancy and delinquency

Dr. Stott's assessments of truants suggest that there is
a high prediction of subsequent delinquency among these
children, but it is not by any means certain that this is
a generally proven fact. One researcher, G. A. Bell, who
published the results of his work in 1963, examined the
attendance records of 492 cases of delinquent behaviour
brought by police to a Belfast magistrates' court. Of these,
eighty-two per cent showed a satisfactory record of attendance, eighteen per cent an irregular or bad record. In
this study Bell began by looking at delinquents to see how
many were truants. A. J. Young, writing just after the
war, a rather critical period, looked at it the other way
round and found no particular association between
delinquency and truants. The truants he examined did
not include significantly more convicted delinquents than
the control group with whom he was comparing them.
Dr. Stott likewise found that of 280 truants, 201 had not
been convicted of any offence.

However, as already pointed out, the very fact a child plays truant makes some kind of anti-social behaviour more likely than would be the case if the child was safely under control in school. The loneliness and isolation of the truant, idleness, hunger and boredom during the day, sets the scene for petty theft or other diversions. The reasons for truancy are not necessarily reasons for delinquent behaviour, but among delinquents are a proportion of children who have played truant and possibly committed a delinquent act while so doing. In the present state of our knowledge it is impossible to assert dogmatically that a truant is a potential delinquent. We need to know the reasons for his truancy before we can fairly make any such assertion, and these reasons vary immensely from one child to another.

Truancy and intelligence

The association of truancy with a low I.Q. has already been noted from Tyerman's work. Other researchers get much the same results from their enquiries, the average I.Q. is low and school attainment poor. However there are factors that have to be taken into consideration when arriving at such a conclusion. This is an instance that illustrates the disadvantage of a small sample of children: it is possible that the locality from which the children are drawn is itself of relatively low standards, and the difference between the I.Q.'s of the truants and non-truants with whom they are being compared is not, in fact, so very significant. The fact that they are missing a proportion of their schooling is certain to handicap them anyway although some researchers have found that truants, when back in school, work up to standard. Where it is true that the majority of a group of truants come from disadvantaged homes in which the parents have little interest in education, there are other factors with which low I.Q. or backwardness in basic subjects could be associated.

Tyerman and Young in their research into school performance and truancy found that backwardness among the truants was more pronounced in spelling and reading than in other subjects. If a child cannot spell or read he is very conscious of the gap between himself and his fellow pupils. His chance of making any real headway in attainment is restricted and his participation in work is inhibited. All this will add up to a sense of isolation and failure which substantially reduces the motivation to attend school. The brighter the child the higher the motivation to attend, the duller the child the less joy there is to be had from attendance.

Among school phobics there is a very strong urge to stand well among fellow pupils, to bolster self-confidence so that the confrontation with others will not be frightening. A sense of failure and futility may well make the phobic reluctant to continue in what seems a useless occupation and to choose something which brings if not joy, at least not the misery-making sense of inferiority associated with the classroom.

On the whole it is difficult to arrive at any hard and fast conclusions about the relationship between I.Q. and truancy, but certain things are quite clear. It is obvious that there are many dull children who are happy at school and well motivated to attend, simply because the school has made a very realistic and educationally expert approach to the whole problem of backwardness, refusing to allow any dull child to feel inferior. There are many ways of doing this, most of which depend heavily upon the personalities of the individual teachers. If dull children do play truant this may possibly be the result of the failure of the school to tackle what is a major educational problem, rather than any personality defect inherent in the children themselves.

Truancy and School Phobias

Truancy and the school

In discussing the reactions of children suffering from school-phobia to the school itself, we have noted that most want to attend school but cannot, for reasons they do not understand. Truants on the other hand appear much more positively opposed to school. Tyerman lists certain aspects of school from which truants are escaping, among these are fear of punishment, scolding or ridicule, compulsory games or showers, shame of backwardness, being ill-dressed, lonely or the subject of some special incident such as physical attack, soiling in the classroom, school examinations, medical or dental examinations. Tyerman refers to such factors as "excuses," but it does seem that any one of them could be very valid reasons for absence.

Several research workers, in spite of repeated assertions by the children themselves about the reasons for their truancy, are reluctant to blame the school. Yet a school is not entirely an impersonal institution governed by inflexible aims and structures. It is very much what the head teacher and staff make it, and this is even more the case in the individual classroom. It is impossible to absolve the schools entirely of blame for truancy. Numbers often militate against the detection of, and special provision for, the less able or the misfit, but this is often a matter of organization which the skilled teacher can overcome. Certainly the attitude of the teacher himself can exercise considerable influence on the reaction of the individual child to school. In the classroom one major motivation is to please the teacher by whatever means are available. But, if the only means acceptable to the teacher is academic achievement, the less able child will immediately sense his complete failure to please unless he does something illegal, like cheating, which, if detected, will have an effect contrary to the one intended. This is a vicious circle from which escape is difficult. If the teacher deliberately seeks out those qualities through which the child can best express himself and then makes clear that these are acceptable, the sense of failure may be avoided. If the teacher claims that he has not the time for this sort of exercise then, regretfully, it is the system and not the child who is at fault. In Dr. Stott's study, "dislike of school" was the most common reason children gave for their absence.

This brings us back to the question of normality and abnormality among children. It has been pointed out by several workers in this area that normal children are not normally truant, and therefore truants are abnormal. But this is an over-simplified statement which avoids the definition of normality. The sum total of the research does not really tell us whether the truant child is a normal child who is the victim of the external circumstances of home and school over which he has no control, other than that of escape, or whether he is a personally maladjusted child suffering from disturbances which cause him to react adversely to what is a relatively normal environment. It is in answer to this quandary that research needs to be directed on a much broader and more substantial scale than has hitherto been the case.

The figures of non-attendance

Although research during the last three years has not added greatly to our knowledge, it has emphasized the need to look more closely at the deeper implications of truancy for both society and the individual. It is not just a simple problem of non-attendance to which "getting them back to school" is the only solution required. Social and educational study needs to be applied to the problem, and such an attempt has been made in Chicago with apparent success.

During the period 1964–72 figures for non-attendance

did not rise substantially. However, in some authorities which were already higher than the national average there has been some increase in the period 1969–72. The national average of attendance is around ninety-one per cent, but in some authorities there was a decline from 89.18 per cent in 1969–70 to 87.81 per cent in 1970–71, the lowest figure for secondary schools being 86.05 per cent. Percentages can be confusing as they give little indication of actual figures. The North West Regional Society of Education Officers helps out with some analyses of actual numbers absent: out of 707,904 on roll, 128,959 were absent some time during the week— 23,806 were absent once, 46,718 were absent twice, 5,577 three times, 16,355 four times, 2,401 five times, 8,085 six times, 1,241 seven times, 5,116 eight times, 940 nine times and 18,720 ten times.

These figures at least provide some numerical idea of the number of children who are actually out of school at some time during the week in a school population of just under 708,000. Further analysis suggests percentages of these figures by reason for absence. In sixty-three per cent of the cases illness of the child was believed to be the cause, this figure could possibly be increased by a further nine per cent. Eighteen per cent were kept back by parents for one reason or another including three per cent who were on holiday; five per cent overslept and so were late and five per cent were truant. Thus, of the total 129,000 absent at some time during the week, some 6,450 were playing truant. This is quite a significant number of children in one region who, in one way or another, needed some social or educational treatment. A proportion were, of course, receiving treatment of some sort in special education or remedial classes in ordinary schools, but the problem remains, demanding much more information and research before any real attack upon it can be made on a national scale.

Summary

Because statistics can be misleading and often difficult to evaluate, research can likewise be misleading, not because it is invalid as a piece of work in its own right, but because it is partial and limited in scope. From the work that has been done certain features of the truant emerge: he tends to come from a poor home background, to have little motivation to attend school because of low attainment, his parents do not take an interest in his education, he is subjected to inconsistent discipline and/or corporal punishment, in personality he tends to be a "loner" and to appear unhappy, such friends as he has are outside the school rather than in it, during periods of truancy he may commit anti-social acts or petty larceny.

In all the research there is much description, but little that suggests such clear causes for the condition of the child which could make treatment possible. The definitions of truancy vary from one worker to another, and almost all consider it a form of deviant behaviour indicating personality defects.

Treatment of truants has been attempted by several education authorities. The form of treatment has been social rather than clinical; the appointment of social or welfare workers actually in schools working closely with teachers, children and parents has been the general pattern. This does indeed seem the first step, but others are necessary. A close examination of the relationship of the truant child to the teacher and to the aims and attitudes of the school is necessary. If the school cannot accommodate the child a change of school may produce some improvement; if home and school are so completely at loggerheads that no real progress is possible a residential school may be the answer. Above all the careful examination of the individual child, with a sympathetic attitude towards his own view of himself, is essential if the roots of the trouble are to be found and dealt with early in the complaint.

Truancy differs from school-phobia in the sort of reaction that it elicits from those connected with the child. The truant is seldom vocal, articulate, clinging or violently protesting; this sort of behaviour demands attention and, if pursued long enough, will get it. The truant is more often quietly miserable, and his first demanding outcry may be a delinquent act rather than a vocal request. The one warning that comes through loud and clear from the research work that has been done is that absence from school for reasons other than illness is not just a superficial problem of discipline, but a demand for attention that it is the duty of the educational services to provide.

2

Patterns of Absence

WHEN a particular pattern of behaviour becomes the normal pattern for society as a whole, anyone who does not conform stands out like a sore thumb, an embarrassment to his immediate family, a problem for those whose task it is to set the pattern and a further problem for those who must determine the penalties, if any, of failing to conform. In recent years we have seen many established patterns of behaviour challenged: patterns of personal appearance and personal behaviour, styles of family life and attitudes to work. In most cases these are adult decisions, concerned only with the adoption of a sort of behaviour which depends upon a socially permissible individual choice, however deviant that choice may be from the choice of the majority. Only rarely do these types of deviation fall into the category of illegal actions.

Attendance at school, for all children over five years of age, is not only a normal pattern of social behaviour it is also a legal necessity. Failure to attend school for any reason, apart from illness or other constraint beyond the control of parents or children, is an illegal act with recognized penalties. Parents, generally speaking, want their children to attend school for many reasons: it is necessary for the child's future, it is good for his present development, it is the normal thing for all normal children to do. Failure to go suggests possible abnormality, and no one wants to be, or appear to be, abnormal, or be thought to have an abnormal child. Children too, on the whole, want to go to school. They do not have such strong feelings about their future or the social susceptibilities of their parents, but they enjoy the company, they like learning if it is presented as an enjoyable occupation, and they, like their parents, like to do what everyone does. Motivation is present in both parents and children, and yet some children fail to attend of their own volition, some are deliberately prevented from attending by their parents and some, in spite of both themselves and their parents wanting them to attend, find themselves unable to do so.

The precise number of children who do not attend for reasons other than illness are difficult to discover. In 1965 the Education Welfare Officers National Association carried out a survey to discover the true incidence of non-attendance. At the time of the survey it seemed that about two per cent of all absences were due to children playing truant without the knowledge of their parents. It is now suggested by some authorities that in large urban areas this figure is considerably higher, it may vary between five and ten per cent of all children at any one time, although at least half this number will have been absent for less than five days at a stretch. For the present it is important to realize that truancy, in the widest sense, presents a very real problem for several groups of people.

I began by referring to patterns of social behaviour, rather than compulsory behaviour enforceable by law. This is an important distinction, because education is more than a legal necessity like paying income tax or stamping an insurance card, it is very much a social activity. Failure to participate in this activity strongly suggests some social defect that needs attention, as well as individual problems that may need treatment. We have, therefore, a social setting for truancy in which it is necessary to look for social causes for the children's behaviour, causes sufficiently strong to militate against the pressures to conform.

There is also a personal problem. As I have indicated, there is a small proportion of children who want to go to school but cannot, who find themselves with all the usual motivations for conformity, for learning, for companionship, and yet are unable to make the transition from home to school.

Three types of school refusal

After this brief introduction to the background of absence from school we can look in closer detail at the three main types of refusal to attend. Illness has been excluded from these descriptions because it is a normal form of absence, does not arouse curiosity or "interest" from the parent's social circle and is, therefore, "conforming" behaviour.

Having excluded illness, there are three types of school refusal, each of which must be looked at separately but which are not always as clear cut in diagnosis as might seem possible at first sight.

First is truancy without the knowledge of the parents. This is the most common form of refusal and can arise from a wide variety of causes. But it is important to remember at the outset that though it is a relatively common activity, and may be indulged in at some time in the school career of many children, it is still a non-conforming activity. Most children want to conform in the main activities of living and among young children non-conformity is seldom a deliberate, thought-out choice. If a child occasionally absents himself for a specific purpose, such as attending a football match or the local appearance of a favourite pop star, a deliberate alternative to school has been chosen and the event will probably not be repeated. In such circumstances it would be much better if the parents had recognized the child's strong desire to attend the other event. Then, having realized the conflict, either accompanied him in an open, if reprehensible, breach of school rules, or taken him personally to school, making it clear that the alternative activity was "not on" and that disobedience would result in firm disciplinary action.

Such occasions as these need cause no anxiety to anyone. Much more disturbing is the child who stays away frequently without any apparent reason, other than that he does not want to go to school. He will get up at the usual time, dress and leave home as though making quite normally for school. He will likewise return home at the appropriate time, as though straight from school; his parents may not be aware for some time that he has been playing truant. Much will, of course, depend upon the school's attitude to his absence. For a time he may be able to provide plausible excuses which may be accepted but, sooner or later, he will be referred to the Educational Welfare Officer who may contact the family and make the parents aware of the situation. The child's behaviour under these circumstances will be relatively purposeless. He will pass the day as far away from both school and home as he can get, he may mooch idly around the shops, visit friends to whom he can tell a reasonable story for his non-attendance at school, go to large, busy places, like airports or stations, where people are unlikely to recognize him, or pursue some occupation of his own which will not attract attention. There is always the danger that he may find idleness boring and drift into delinquent habits; if he frequents a particular area of the town he may well find himself under the observation of the police and be picked up in the occasional sweeps that they make.

Two examples of children in this situation will illustrate the issues raised for both the parents and others responsible for them during school hours.

Janet came to the attention of a social worker through

one of the Educational Welfare Officers, who, working
in close contact with the local social services department,
realized that her family was already being visited by that
department. Janet was twelve years old, reasonably intelligent and of tidy appearance. Her father had deserted
the home eleven months before she first absented herself
from school. Her mother knew nothing about these
absences, seeing Janet off at the usual time in the morning and greeting her when she returned home around
4.30 p.m. At first she was absent only about once a week
when, she said, her mother had kept her at home to look
after the younger children, while she did the shopping.
Her absences gradually increased until she was missing
three days in succession. On her return to school the head
questioned her, decided her answers were very inadequate
and reported the matter to the E.W.O. with the request
for an early visit to the family. The request was passed
to the social services department and a visit made immediately. Some coaxing was required before Janet
would admit that she had been absent. But when the
social worker told her that all her absences that term had
been noted by the school and reported, she admitted what
she had been doing.

Janet had occupied her time in a variety of ways. On
fine days she called on a family she knew who could be
depended upon to ask no questions if she gave a hand
with the kids. She would take them for a walk or do the
odd bit of shopping. On wet days she would wander
round the shops or go to her friend to help with the
washing. She could, of course, have done these things at
home if she had thought that her mother would agree,
but the home environment was not an accepting one and
Janet knew that her presence there would irritate rather
than please her mother.

After the welfare officer had visited and talked to
Janet several times her attendance improved, but she

persistently declared that she did not like the company of her fellow pupils at school and was unhappy there. The school could not detect any unpleasantness towards Janet on the part of other girls, in spite of careful observation; she seemed a little lonely but was not harassed or teased. The climax of this stage of Janet's trouble came when she stole a bicycle, was picked up by the police, and eventually placed in care. The rest of the story does not immediately relate to her truancy, but illustrates further the symptomatic nature of her early behaviour. Janet was first placed at an assessment centre with its own educational facilities; after a term she was transferred to a community home from which she frequently absconded. At fourteen she is back home, under a supervision order, and attending school once more.

A second truant, sometimes with but more often without his mother's knowledge, was Patrick, the eldest child of a one-parent family. Mild truancy was of long standing, but after his father's desertion, when Pat was fourteen, it became far more persistent and an anxiety to both the school and the social services. The chief sign of disturbance in an otherwise pleasant and easy-going boy was a degree of untruthfulness that went beyond simple excuses. It was difficult at times to tell if Patrick himself realized when he was telling the truth and when it was sheer imagination. Sometimes he would stay at home with his mother's connivance, but at other times he would set off for school, catch the school bus, reach school but get no further than the gate. He would wander around the town all day and hitch-hike home to arrive back at about the right time. Pat was a "loner" and seemed to have few friends other than local shop-keepers who knew him well. Unfortunately the enforced idleness got him into trouble, for after some suspicion of shop-lifting he was finally caught and reported to the police. The social worker concerned with the family felt it might be a good disciplinary measure for Pat to be taken to court, and he was duly placed on probation.

In both these cases the children showed early signs of truancy without parental knowledge, which later led them into mild delinquency as the result of their isolation and idleness. Both children came from one-parent families with a background of family disturbance with which, superficially at least, their truancy might be associated. Although Janet made friends with another family in a similar situation to her own, neither child made any contact with other children of similar ages.

Gang truancy is not uncommon, but in most of the cases examined (thirty covering a period of three years) this is very hard to substantiate among persistent truants. A group of children may absent themselves for a fishing expedition or just because it is a nice day and a boring lesson is coming up. But this is rare. Police reports suggest that in the more anonymous urban areas truant children will gang up for a shop-lifting expedition.

However, generally speaking, the characteristics displayed by Janet and Patrick are typical and repeat themselves again and again. A ten-year-old boy went daily to the park and played on the swings all day, only joining his fellow pupils as they came out of school. It was a week before he was found out and the matter reported to his parents. Even after considerable efforts by both parents to ensure his attendance at school, he would slip away after break or lunch and his mother would know where to find him. He is at present attending the Child Guidance Clinic and perhaps has a chance of returning to normality before he, like many others, begins to drift into trouble.

The second category of truancy is the deliberate withholding of the child from school by one or both parents, usually the mother. To keep a child away from school

29

when he is in good health and able to attend is, of course, illegal. I shall look at the legal situation in more detail later, but, whatever the cause, such action will inevitably involve the welfare officer, the social services or, as a last resort, the courts. Very few parents, relative to the total number of children so withheld, are in fact brought to court; the causes are usually of a sort that demand help for the family, the mother or the child, and legal action is not the way to tackle the problem. If legal action is taken it is, more often than not, done so as a form of shock treatment which often proves effective in steering the home to a more responsible form of behaviour.

The reasons for withholding a child are very varied, some are inexcusably selfish, some appear selfish but have deep laid psychological reasons that have to be discovered and dealt with, some are attitudes to life which are born of poor education, poor environment or long histories of family disturbance.

Margaret was twelve when I first met her doing a local paper round. To do this it was necessary to get up at about 6.30 a.m., as she had to dress and feed a younger sister before she was allowed to leave the house. After her paper round she had to get breakfast for her father who did casual labour on building sites. By the time Margaret's morning chores were complete it was often after school time, and her mother would use this as an excuse for keeping her away from school for the whole day to help her with the washing and housework. Late in the afternoon Margaret would wander towards the school to meet her friends as they came out. She was kept from school, on average, one day a week. If her father was out of work she might be at home several days at a stretch because, as her mother remarked, "There's more needs doing with him around the house."

I called on Margaret's mother to discuss this unsatisfactory situation, for Margaret was, in any case, a year below the legal age for doing a paper round. Persuasion and threats were equally ineffective with Margaret's parents. Though repentant for a few weeks, a spell of father's unemployment would start matters up again, and although the paper round was dropped in the interest of Margaret's health, it was not until her father was taken to court that matters began to improve.

The family were neither particularly hard up nor heartless towards their children. They were disorganized and thoughtless and mother, with more small children to care for than she could cope with, stayed in bed as long as possible and made a drudge of the eldest daughter. In such circumstances recourse to the law was the only means of administering the sort of treatment likely to make an impression.

Peter, aged six, was a very different sort of case. He began school well and, having attended a playgroup for a year, found no difficulty in leaving his mother. He was a lively and attractive child who was a pleasure to have in the reception class. The trouble began in his second year when he was unaccountably absent for three days. Enquiries by his school elicited the explanation that he was "off colour" and so mother had kept him at home. This was reasonable in a small child and was accepted on the first two occasions. On the third prolonged absence the school felt concerned and asked for a social worker to call at the home and make some tactful enquiries. Peter had shown some signs of distress and withdrawal, and his teacher suspected that circumstances at home might be the cause. It was soon discovered that the first absence had coincided with the father's desertion of his family. Mother was very distressed, and found it impossible at times to part with Peter who now seemed her only reason for living and her one escape from the acute loneliness that she was experiencing. Quite a long period of counselling was needed before some stability was re-established, and his mother would accept Peter's absence from home during school hours.

The third category of absence comprises those instances in which, for some apparently unknown reason, a child cannot bring himself to attend school, although he appears to want to go and both the parents are anxious to get him there. This condition has been described frequently as school-phobia, though it is questionable whether there is, in fact, any particular phobic characteristic involved.

Nine-year-old Robin had to change schools because his parents moved to another part of the country. He began school quite satisfactorily, although with a reluctance which seemed natural enough in a young child being introduced to new surroundings and strange faces. The first term went quite well, though Robin's performance in class was well below what might have been expected from previous experience. He could read perfectly satisfactorily before leaving his first school, but now appeared to have difficulties and was marked down in this part of his work, although no sign of retrogression appeared when he was reading at home. The second term opened with, again, reluctance but no demonstrative refusal. It was after the half-term holiday that real trouble began. The signs usually associated with this condition became very apparent, stomach pains and prolonged periods in the toilet before setting out for school and complaints of headaches and nausea. On the third morning after the half-term he refused to enter the school building, and created such a scene that his mother took him home. At home he became quite normal, no pains and no hysterics, but equally no rational explanation of his behaviour. In the ensuing weeks constant efforts were made to take him back but each time, as soon as he approached the school building, the same symptoms were renewed. Eventually a change of school was tried. After much persuasion Robin consented to attend a form two years below his own age, with a form master of quite exceptional ability and sympathy. He would not, however, stay to the mid-day meal and his mother met and took him out for this. He spent the rest of that term and the whole of the next with the younger age group. Stability was slowly re-established, and when the school insisted that he joined his own age group there was only a forty-eight hour period of protest and then no further trouble. Robin is now eleven and well settled, although at times he seems on the edge of refusal he overcomes it under pressure of parental refusal "to have any further nonsense." There are many facets of Robin's case which I shall look at later when considering treatment of school-phobia in more detail, for the present it is the symptoms which concern us.

One research worker has isolated six characteristics which may be associated with this trouble and these all applied to Robin's condition:

1. The child's parents cannot get him to school.
2. He seems anxious about things which he should be able to cope with at his age and stage of learning and development.
3. There are physical symptoms associated with a disturbed condition of anxiety.
4. The child appears fearful, inactive and withdrawn. (This was rather less true of Robin who was normal enough at home though found any prolonged period of concentration very difficult, a not unusual feature of children of his age.)
5. He shows violent signs of fear of school when actually approaching the building.
6. He comes from a home where education is regarded as important.

These characteristics distinguish the child suffering from school-phobia from the child who plays truant without parental knowledge. But the exact dividing line between the two is very difficult to discover, especially when the two conditions are looked at as precipitating causes rather than simply in terms of effects and behaviour.

A second case, with slight variations on the first, is that of Gerald aged eleven. Gerald is now undergoing a second period of refusal. The first occurred when, at seven and a half, he would show all the rather alarming signs of terror on approaching the building. Each day throughout that year Gerald would kick and scream and have to be dragged into school by his teacher. Once there, with the trauma of parting over, he settled down for the day. A year later things became normal again. There was no trouble until he was eleven and a half, when physical symptoms—tummy pains—began, followed by absolute refusal to attend, although he declares no special objection to school itself and has plenty of friends. He is of good intelligence and school reports are favourable. He sleeps well and is normal in behaviour when at home. His periods of anxiety are confined to the immediate pre-school time; frequently he will lock himself in the toilet until this period is over and his mother agrees to let him stay at home, for he is now too big to be dragged to school. Gerald is, at present, under treatment at the Child Guidance Clinic at his mother's request.

The expression "school-phobia" may be used to distinguish such cases as those of Robin and Gerald from the other types of truancy described, but it is not in fact a very satisfactory definition. In the first place it suggests that the cause of the complaint lies in the school, which is not by any means demonstrated by research. There may be complementary factors in the school situation which aggravate or even precipitate the condition, but there is very little evidence to suggest that these are causative factors. In the second place the word "phobia" is a technical term used by psycho-analysts to describe a condition of fear brought about by association of a place, or person, with a repressed experience or anxiety. Occasionally a case arises which does seem to be of this sort, but more often than not the association is with an experience at home rather than at school.

Some research workers prefer the expression "school refusal," since this is at least descriptive of the condition and does not raise the questions attached to technical terms. "School-phobia," however, is now so widely used for this condition that it seems unwise to discard it at this stage. School refusal could also be applied, quite aptly, to other cases of children wilfully refusing to attend school for conscious reasons to which the characteristics of a "phobia" would not apply. I shall, therefore, retain the more traditional terms of truancy, withholding and school-phobia for the three groups of behaviour which I have described. Common factors between them may emerge from the examination of causes and treatment, but in terms of symptoms they are three useful divisions for the one problem of non-attendance.

3

What Are They
Afraid Of?

IN Chapter 2 the problem of defining school-phobia was mentioned, but anyone who has watched the behaviour of a child suffering from school-phobia can have no doubt whatever about the element of fear in such behaviour. The fear, however, takes many different forms and is displayed in one way or another both at home and at school as well as on the way to school.

At fourteen and a half, Jane was still suffering from a "phobia" which made her incapable of attending school with any real regularity. She was afraid of going to school, looking at her school uniform or even seeing other children in school uniform. When persuaded to attend school for one hour a day she was afraid of being sick, and insisted on sitting near the door so that she could easily rush out to the toilet if she needed to; she was afraid of being shut in anywhere where there seemed no immediate way of escape.

The physical symptoms accompanying school-phobia, such as the ones Jane showed, are also indicators of fear. Nausea, stomach pains, lack of concentration and sleeplessness all show the presence of fear. But although these symptoms accompany an exaggerated reluctance to attend school, the fear is not necessarily directed towards the school itself. Some children, once in school, are, unlike Jane, perfectly happy and will go through the day without apparent fear or anxiety and return home declaring what a happy day they have had. But the next morning the symptoms will all reappear and the child will make the "going to school" process as painful and traumatic as possible. There is such a wide variety of behaviour patterns between truancy, with few or no symptoms of physical illness, and school-phobia, in which a child may stop eating and show signs of severe physical deterioration, that some researchers are very loath to put in dividing lines that mark off one group from another. However, there is clearly, right through the whole range of cases of refusal to attend school, a fear of—or aversion to—school, which demands attention. The problem must be seen as a whole, and not solely in the light of the most severely disturbed children or the most anxious parents. There has been a tendency to dismiss the simple truant as a mild discipline problem, and yet persistent truancy may well be a sign of emotional disturbance just as deep and damaging to the child as the much more apparent symptoms displayed by cases clearly categorized as "phobic." It cannot be stressed enough that, in children, abnormal behaviour, in which symptoms are suppressed and explanations superficial or unreal, should be taken quite as seriously as behaviour accompanied by evident distress and overt symptoms.

It is worth beginning an answer to the question "What are they afraid of?" by reminding ourselves of some of the epithets applied to the children. Loneliness, isolation and aimlessness are characteristics applied to many truants. Anxiety, depression, timidity and panic afflict many of those classified as school-phobics.

The school is the object of aversion and fear, but these conditions are deeply rooted within the child himself and what he perceives in the school is the projection of his fears rather than any objective condition that teacher or parent can isolate. Indeed, it is significant that in careful questioning of the children there is little or no evidence that they are averse to particular teachers or particular routines or activities at school. Occasionally a child will complain that a teacher has shouted at him or a classmate bullied or harassed him in some way, but on investigation these complaints are difficult to substantiate. Such situations, when they do actually occur, are much more likely to be precipitating factors in the child's refusal, rather than causative ones. It is quite possible that a timid child will play truant if he is afraid of others ganging up against him in the playground, but normal observation of children at play soon reveals instances of this behaviour which even timid children manage to cope with as part, albeit an unpleasant one, of school life.

There are many pressures and tensions in school which children have to learn to cope with, but, with the help of his teachers, the normal child does cope and to opt out of the situation is abnormal behaviour which has deeper causes than the pressures of the school day.

Isolation and a sense of loneliness in children immediately suggest some defect in the early stages of the child's upbringing. Children who are loved and well cared for by those around them in the early years of infancy develop a sense of security and confidence in relation to the outside world that enables them to make satisfactory social progress throughout the school years. This sense of innate worth and self-confidence is what enables even the timid or physically slight child to stand up to the rough and tumble of school relationships. The child whose infancy has lacked this foundation will experience difficulty in making social contacts with other children and adults from the reception class onwards. If he is fortunate the deficiencies of the past may be made up in some measure by a good teacher, by an accepting atmosphere in the school and by natural childhood resilience; everything will turn upon the degree and the kind of the early deficiencies. If he is unfortunate the experience of being thrown into the throng of strange, noisy and possibly aggressive classmates will produce an aversion which will isolate him and force him, as time goes on, to seek only his own company and to fashion his behaviour on his estimate of himself; seeing himself as "not wanted" or "not worthy." The company of others will not be wanted and not be worthy. So the self-image is projected upon the world outside in spite of its objective "worthiness." So the fear of the school may be a fear of what it implies —an acceptance of his own worth which in fact he does not or cannot admit.

As he grows older the same child will have added to the social problem an academic one, a problem of achievement and of failure. But this is closely bound up with parental and school attitudes which will be considered later.

Anxiety and depression are often used as descriptive of school-phobia cases. The characteristics occur as much at home as at school. The line between fear and anxiety is not easy to draw, but a distinction may be made between the fear of some specific external object and a condition of anxiety within the child which does not seem to attach to any particular object or specific situation. In such cases the real object or situation is suppressed or unknown to the child. In school-phobia it is the school and objects associated with it that give rise to the anxiety or bring it to the surface, but they are not necessarily its real cause.

We are accustomed to describing children who show signs of emotional disturbance as maladjusted, implying that, for some reason, the child is failing to satisfactorily adjust his own needs and desires to the supply of those things available to him. In theory we might say a well adjusted child has a plentiful supply of what he requires, or that he has managed to reduce his demands in accordance with the limitations of the source of supply. A rather better word to describe the situation is disequilibrium. This word has a quantitative content which is a necessary factor in the child's growth. Just as the body needs a certain quantity of the right nutrients if it is to remain healthy, so the child's growing personality requires a certain quantity of love and care from those around him, a certain quantity of respect that ensures an adequate recognition of worth, a certain amount of acceptance that will give an understanding of belonging, home and family. The balance of childhood needs with familial and environmental supply establishes an equilibrium. It is often a very delicate and complex balance in which many people and physical conditions play a part, but the whole process of development is so rooted in these inter-personal relationships that, under normal circumstances, everybody works to maintain the balance.

Severe disequilibrium is a condition of severe deprivation. It has fairly clear indicators, such as lack of communication with the outside world, withdrawal, unnatural aggressiveness, the erection of barriers of indifference, learning difficulties, and physical symptoms such as stunted growth and sleeplessness. But the child will fight the disequilibrium in whatever ways are available. School is a secure place with a system, a timetable and a discipline of orderliness. Teachers are generally accepting people and, if time permits, affectionate and helpful to the obviously distressed. It is not, therefore, surprising that, on the whole, deprived children like and appreciate school and do not try to avoid it. Indeed school does much to help such children redress the balance of deprivation. It cannot be a substitute for inadequate parental care, but it is another sort of weight which can be put on the supply side of the scales to balance the child's needs.

Research into school-phobia does not reveal any significant association between the broken or deficient home, and the condition of "phobia" refusal to attend school.

In a recent study of fifty-five school refusers only two were from broken homes; other surveys have shown a similar lack of connection between the two conditions. If a child from a broken home is also suffering from school-phobia it is most probable that he would have suffered from it even if the home had not broken up. It is, of course, possible that a single incident in the home life of the child could have precipitated the condition, but it would be unlikely to have been the root cause of it.

To probe the real nature of the child's fear we must go much deeper than the overt evidence of inter-familial strife or breakdown, deeper than the parental neglect or rejection of the child. These undoubtedly produce stress and anxiety, but they do not often produce school-phobia.

One of the characteristics of "phobic" children that frequently occurs in case histories is their apparent anxiety about sharing the company of children of their own age. The most significant factor about school is the simple and obvious one that it contains a large number of children in conditions of concentration that do not exist elsewhere. Association with other children is forced upon the school attender. Children refusing to attend school will often accept alternatives without any demur. One eleven-year-old boy from a happy family environment exhibited extreme symptoms of phobia on approaching the school building and resisted all attempts to get him out of his mother's car when they arrived. But he was perfectly content to sit all day in the public library and work at whatever was set him. In some respects he probably covered more ground academically than if he had been a school attender! Before being finally reintegrated into school life he spent several hours a day helping the school secretary or doing his work in the comparative privacy of her office; suggestions that he should attend games, at least with his age group, produced such panic that the idea was dropped. Recovery for this child was a long, slow process spread over two years.

Inability to mix with the peer group suggests a gross lack of self-confidence in the child, which, in turn, suggests that no significant self-image has emerged in the process of development. The fear of such children is directed upon the encounter between their non-self and the real selves of all the other children with whom school compels them to associate. At home they are secure because their real identity is rooted in the duality of the mother/child relationship. The real and deep seated fear lies in this absence of any adequate self to stand up against other selves. In the early stages of integration these children will try to make their way into the group by over-submissiveness, bribery, boasting or other compensations that appear to them to establish their identity before their fellows. This is often so, in spite of any intellectual or physical advantages they will be able to display. They cannot believe they have anything of their own to offer.

But lack of self-confidence is not always limited to the school situation and is frequently shown at home as well. Not only do such children show abnormal behaviour symptoms but they are also frequently withdrawn, refusing to go out and insist on staying close to mother. They may be defiant and rude to their mothers but still find intense difficulty in breaking away from them. The mothers themselves are often neurotic or insecure, perhaps in their marital relationships or as a result of their childhood experiences. They frequently project their anxiety upon the children. In many instances removal from home to a residential school has brought about improvement as it has permitted the child to develop a personality of his own, or has compelled him into so doing. In some case histories a closer relationship with the father has effected change. It would seem that this has the effect of breaking the symbiotic relationship between mother and child and facilitates independent development.

Some examples of children suffering from school-phobia will illustrate the points I have made. It is significant that although each case may illustrate some of these points, it is very difficult to discover isolated cases which show so substantial a number of symptoms that they can be regarded as a distinctive syndrome.

Sarah's disturbance seemed to begin at the age of thirteen years and nine months, when her mother ordered the destruction of a dog to which Sarah was very attached. She became depressed and sullen about the loss of the dog, and also disturbed by the hostility she felt towards her mother who was the cause of the loss. This feeling of hostility made her feel guilty. Her school refusal was associated with an acute fear of her schoolmates who, she felt, were all against her. She experienced a complete loss of self-confidence. Her emotional upset coincided with the beginning of her periods which she could not easily accept, describing this experience as "awful." Sarah was the youngest child of the family and, for practical purposes, an only child. Thus a combination of circumstances occurring at the puberal stage of development precipitated refusal to attend school and a decline in standards of work. Sarah worked through her problems in six months, returning to school regularly and regaining her work standard.

Dorothy experienced difficulties of school attendance when she transferred from primary to secondary school just after her eleventh birthday. She appeared both anxious and depressed, and complained of abdominal pains and buzzing in her head. She became very withdrawn; not only did she refuse to attend school but also refused to leave the house. She was very clinging towards her mother, but at the same time showed defiance and disregard of her mother's efforts to help or persuade her to make some social effort outside the home. The whole tenor of the relationship between mother and daughter was strained and difficult though father, to whom Dorothy was very attached, managed her quite well. Eventually, Dorothy began to take an interest in some of her friends from junior school and in six months transferred successfully to the grammar school.

Ann started quite satisfactorily at secondary school. But in spite of a high intelligence rating she complained that the work was too hard for her. At the same time she complained of aches and pains which were difficult to isolate or define. She became anxious and depressed about her work. Her refusal to attend school was precipitated by seeing a dog run over by a car. Her anxiety was apparent in an over-attention to time and detail and a constantly expressed worry about her mother when Ann was away from her. Mother was a nervous person who had had an unhappy childhood and tended to over-protect and over-mother Ann in her anxiety that this past unhappiness should not affect her daughter.

Ann found the preoccupation with sex of girls at her secondary school abhorrent, and would have nothing to do with their discussions of boys, cosmetics and clothes. The death of a relative increased her depression and she brooded on death in general and her own in particular, and this became yet another cause of fear. Ann's recovery from this unfortunate series of circumstances began when her mother started discussing her own childhood and the difficulties she had experienced. As a girl of high intelligence Ann began to rationalize some of her anxieties and to understand them. Relationships between mother and daughter improved and became more mature. Ann regained her self-confidence and emotional stability, returning to normal school attendance after nine months' treatment.

These three cases show some of the symptoms already

discussed and some of the types of fear that depress and cause deep anxiety. The precipitating events are often of little importance in themselves, but bring to the surface some facet of the underlying disturbance. In each case the mother-child relationship is a significant background feature of the emotional condition and constitutes a problem which must be resolved before freedom and self-confidence can be regained. To describe this relationship as the cause of the disturbance is to make too definitive a statement of its place in the overall problem, since many children with very difficult parent-child relationships do not necessarily react with school-phobia.

One of the interesting features of research into school-phobia has been the wide distribution of age over a number of studies. The children extend from five to seventeen years of age, but the numbers of children referred for treatment rise around the onset of puberty. The difficulty of drawing conclusions from the age distribution lies in the variations from one study to another of the method of selection or referral. One writer studied fifty-five children and found a mean age of seven years and nine months, another examining fifty children found forty-two over nine years of age. There seems, however, to be a relationship in many cases between school refusal and the onset of puberty. This may be, like so many other factors in the generally disturbed condition of the child, a precipitating rather than a causative factor; sleeplessness, unrest and sometimes depression often afflict children between eleven and thirteen.

In attempting to probe the child's fear during the period of disturbance, age is important. There are critical ages in the gradual process of physical and mental development, there are also critical ages which are determined by social circumstances. For children the ages of transfer from one educational establishment to another are critical. In conditions of educational reorganization these ages vary widely from area to area. Primary school from five to eleven offers two critical ages, one when starting school and one when transferring to secondary school. There is also a change at seven, either from an infant to a junior school or from one department to another within the same school. Middle schooling will slightly change these critical ages to eight or nine and twelve or thirteen. Nursery schooling, from about three years and six months, will ease the entry problem or make it earlier.

Children are undoubtedly nervous about change, and refusal at such a period of "settling in" would seem a strong likelihood in children who, for other reasons, may have a predisposition to "phobia." Even a new form, with new faces of classmates and staff, may arouse seemingly exaggerated fears in a child, the fear, always close to every human personality, of not being able to cope with the unknown. Many children deliberately slack off in their work in order to avoid being moved up and losing a less able friend who may be left behind, or having to face new faces that are threatening to a security built up in the old form.

There is also the important element of achievement which persists in every educational system, however much that system may try to avoid the ill effects of excessive competition in a society of mixed and various abilities. The fear of failure is very real in children, indeed it extends, in its effects, into adult life. There is fear of social as well as academic failure, the frantic efforts of some children to shine before their fellows at all costs leads to all kinds of bizarre behaviour. It is, however, questionable whether the fear of not achieving will lead, unaided, to a determination to opt out of the situation. Under-achieving children form a constant ten per cent or more of any non-selective school and they do not suffer from school-phobia. The factors contributing to under-achievement are different from those which appear to contribute to

47

school-phobia, and it is undoubtedly a fact that many children in the latter category have quite a high ability rating and little cause to fear failure. Truancy, however, is more frequent among the children of low performance. But since such children are by no means the odd-men-out in their school setting, we must look for the root causes of truancy elsewhere than in their educational performance.

We began this chapter with the question "What are they afraid of?" We have examined a fair range of fears, causes of anxiety and depression and external events which have triggered disturbance manifesting itself in an inability to attend school. We have seen how difficult it is to distinguish between those things in the child's experience which set off the condition of "phobia" and those which may be deeply laid contributing causes. Many of the cases examined show defects in the mother/child relationship which are inhibiting the emergence of an independent personality in the child, but even in these instances it is clear that these defects do not always result in school-phobia. We must, therefore, assume two possible conditioning situations for those children, either there is a set of circumstances which produce a high risk of emotional disturbance manifesting itself in, among other behaviour patterns, school-phobia; or we must assume a genetic predisposition to an extended period of dependence which, when combined with other predisposing factors in the environment, results in disturbance. Unfortunately genetic factors are exceedingly difficult to isolate and we must await much more research before reaching any certainty in this area.

With the knowledge and understanding at our disposal there are some useful aspects of children's development that we can examine, so increasing our chances of helping them. These are the family relationships which are so influential throughout the whole of childhood, and the away-from-home relationships which represent the child's out-reach beyond home and are the means of shaping and influencing the emerging personality. The child's desire to establish equilibrium between his needs and desires and the capacity of his environment to meet or allow them is the movement towards maturity for which the ability to establish an equilibrium is essential. The most effective way of helping any child to overcome his fears, and achieve a real degree of emotional stability, is to recognize his needs and so order his environment that he himself can discover within it the means of meeting his needs without having to resort to damaging repression or flight into depression or panic.

4

As the Children See It

CHILDREN'S accounts of their own reasons for not being able to attend school tend to be discounted rather more readily than they warrant. Admittedly fantasy plays a substantial part in any child's explanation of himself, self-analysis and self-understanding are hard enough for adults let alone children, and some degree of rationalization according to what is regarded as reasonable by the individual is only to be expected.

Children know that illness is a reason for not going to school, and therefore the psycho-somatic symptoms that afflict many children in the early stages of school-phobia are an expression of their deeper emotional problems. It is part of the process of treatment to accept the symptoms at their face value, and it would be doing less than justice to the child not to accept them or probe behind them for the disturbances which are closer to the real causes of their distress. Dr. Clyne, in his close study of individual cases brought to his consulting room, illustrates very well this transition in understanding whereby physical illness can be associated with emotional distress and the child, on careful examination, will move from describing the physical symptom to the deeper, emotional one.

May, who was ten years old, came with her mother complaining of pains in her chest and sleeplessness. She expressed a fear of heart trouble and declared that her mother was not concerned about her. On being questioned without her mother present, May admitted that her mother had been ill and that she was afraid of going to school in case something happened to her mother while she was away. There were also stomach aches which kept her away; she wanted to be like her mother and have babies and she would like to marry her father. May had given considerable trouble during her mother's pregnancy seven years earlier and had remained jealous of her younger brother. Her mother had frequently been ill and depressed.

Thus, although the initial complaint that brought mother and child to the doctor faded into the background, May's own description of her condition provided clear indications of the basic causes of distress.

The complaint of sickness, vomiting and diarrhoea is common among many school refusing children. It is very real, and to the child is sufficient reason to keep him at home. The parent is, of course, aware that the refusal precedes the illness and is therefore prone to discount the latter as put on. As parental pressure to attend increases, so does the child's nervous reaction, establishing a vicious circle which often leads to angry exchanges and the child's accusation that the parent does not care or understand. Abdominal pains and actual vomiting and diarrhoea are by far the most common expression of the fear of school attendance. But the child may shift from these to other somatic complaints such as coughs, colds, catarrh, throat or ear complaints. In fact, any form of illness which keeps him at home.

In addition to complaints about pains in their own bodies many children complain about bodily functions, particularly eating. The school meal period may well present problems to the child, and many children during a period of emotional stress about attendance will concentrate upon their need to come home for the mid-day meal. Alan, nine years old, refused to go to school because, he said, he was made to eat the mid-day meal, which made him sick. If he could come home for lunch he would be prepared to attend normally. His mother was at work all day and the house was empty. On further questioning Alan admitted anxiety about his mother's absence and the desire to make sure she was all right during the day. The teacher reported that Alan became increasingly anxious as the lunch interval approached, he was unable to eat his meal and was sometimes scolded for this by one of the dinner ladies who thought him wasteful. Eventually his mother was persuaded to meet him at lunch time and they had sandwiches together in the park. This was sufficient, and Alan's behaviour at school became normal and he left home quite happily each morning.

Abdominal pains or inability to eat are associated with emotional stress or excitement, but the nature of the stress needs investigation; it may be temporary and due to a specific cause which will be removed in the natural course of events, or it may be deep laid, unknown to the child, and need prolonged attention. It has been the subject of medical investigation and the help of the family doctor is always advisable if it appears persistent, although in itself of seemingly minor significance. Dr. Clyne records cases in which doctors had dismissed parental expressions of anxiety with such phrases as "periodic syndrome of childhood." Such diagnosis is not very helpful and quite meaningless to the parent, in most cases an emotional conflict of some kind lies behind the complaint.

Complaints of coughs, catarrh and headaches by children are again frequently associated with emotional upsets. Dr. Clyne records the case of Muriel who, at eleven years old, suffered from such severe headaches she could not attend school. She thought these might be due to her baby brother whom she loved but who had taken some of her mother's love away from her. After discussing this relationship, and her feeling of loss at having to share her mother's affection with her brother, she felt better and was able to return to school.

Children who show symptoms of school-phobia may also develop paranoic attitudes towards the other children at school. They complain that they are teased, laughed at, shunned by their classmates. Richard, who suffered from a prolonged and severe attack of school-phobia at nine years old, complained of having no friends and that no one would play with him. Careful observation by the school staff, who were sincerely worried by Richard's behaviour, found no foundations for these complaints. Once at school he seemed perfectly happy and joined enthusiastically in playground games and seemed to have close contact with several boys both in his own class and outside it. Yet to get him to school was a traumatic experience for all concerned and had eventually to be abandoned. While at home Richard urgently requested the company of other children to play with, and when a friend was invited home Richard would wear him out with his demanding, active play. Richard's disturbance was deep laid and took time to resolve, but his complaint about his school fellows seemed to be a very real fantasy based upon acute anxiety about his non-acceptability among his fellows. A sense of inferiority and fear of failing before others produced a fear which only constant reassurance, both verbal and practical, could gradually dispel.

Children with school-phobia are frequently prepared to go to some lengths to understand themselves, and self-expression on paper has proved useful with the more articulate and reflective children. An eleven-year-old boy from a private school background kept a day to day record of his feelings, noting when he was specially "fed up" or depressed. When compared with the accounts of family affairs given by his mother, it was clear that these periods of depression coincided with periods when his mother was particularly preoccupied by affairs outside the home which took her away for days at a time. He was worried by the thought of the house being empty and shut up, so that he could not go back to it if he wished. His refusal to go to school resulted in further conflict with his mother, who was thus prevented from carrying out what she described as her "duties." Each failed to meet the needs of the other, so the customary vicious circle was established. Considerable case work was needed over some months before a working arrangement could be made with mutual understanding of what really constituted "duty."

Valerie had suffered from bouts of school-phobia for a prolonged period of her school life. At fifteen she was still an anxious and introverted girl in spite of a high level of school attainment and considerable success in "overcoming" her difficulties of attendance. The social worker who had been visiting her home regularly for several months had established a good relationship with her and persuaded her to write about her feelings and reflections. The result was a long and detailed diary of events which brings out with remarkable clarity many of the points made above about the physical symptoms of school-phobia, as well as other points from which much can be learned of the real experience to which children are subject in these times of anxiety and depression. Valerie's account of herself is given here at length because it reveals so well a real experience; as she says, you need to experience it before you can really understand:

"I never really stayed at one school for more than two years, somehow I just got into a rut with the routine, teachers and friends and moved on. The most I ever spent at any one school was a private one for two and a half years and only left because it had to close down through lack of funds. The present school is now a state one, at first I found it rather strange, probably because of the streaming, I was always used to the brains and the dunces being mixed up together, and the fact of being in a class with boys. For two and a half years I had been segregated with girls. The first item to strike me about this fact was at the end of a lesson the teacher would say 'girls first.' I found this rather a novelty. At school I was never actually a leader but was very jolly and didn't find it difficult to make friends. I was very conscientious about my work and at my previous school somehow managed to come first in the class, hardly surprising as there were only twelve girls in the class. After the private school closed down and my friends all split up, some to state schools and some not, when I told them I decided to go state they said I could probably get into the 'O' level stream and started my new school with this idea in mind. I was a little bit disappointed when they put me in a CSE class ... My first year was the best. I was enthusiastic for everything going on, the school was across the road and I could see my house from some of the classrooms. The school said they were thinking of putting me into the top stream but thought it best to leave me where I was because I worried a lot about the work. For the first term of my second year all was fine. But then I noticed I was different from the others, not physically, I suppose I looked a bit older, but mentally. My classmates didn't share the same interests as me, I was mad about pop groups, but no one in my class liked the same ones as me; I knew people in the top streams who did but when I talked to them I felt stupid and inferior. Also I liked books but no one in my form had ever heard of the authors I liked. I never considered myself better than anybody else but just different. At the end of the day I felt as if I could do more, as if I wanted more. I had this strange sensation that my mind was growing smaller instead of expanding to take in more knowledge. By now I was not quite so enthusiastic about school. I first noticed something was not quite right in the morning. I was never all that good at getting up and was always a late riser and never bothered with breakfast. I woke up one morning and had a horrible sick feeling in my stomach, but I got up and went to school as usual as it was my birthday. I went into school with a green face saying to myself 'you can't be sick on your birthday.' I arrived just in time to be violently sick in the toilets, immediately I wished I hadn't come. During the morning it wore off. The next day exactly the same thing happened. Unfortunately it was assembly so rather than go and tell somebody I felt sick I went in. I was first in and sat near the front. Suddenly in the middle of a hymn I wanted to be sick. I had this claustrophobic feeling and wanted to get out quick, but how walk out with 600 eyes on you or be sick with 600 eyes on you? I concentrated and stuck it out to the end, that was the longest half-hour of my life. The next lesson was needlework and people were walking in and out of the room all the time so I could easily vanish unnoticed to the toilets. With this thought my sickness vanished and I carried on as normal. For the whole of the week it was the same, but now I went and told the head about it. Mum took me to the doc who gave me some tablets which stopped me from being sick. I took them for about a year except weekends and hols. I only felt sick when I went to school. I didn't blame any one including the doctor who laughed sarcastically as I suppose it did look as if I didn't like going to school, which in turn meant I didn't like work which made me look lazy."

(At the end of her second year there was further discussion about her promotion to the 'O' level class, but the school decided that her health was against this. The decision coincided with some school reorganization that put the two lower streams together leaving the top stream untouched. Valerie was bitterly disappointed at not being moved up, she felt "bored and frustrated.")

"By now I was going around in a 'click' of girls in our class, they were the most intelligent ones in our form and I suppose the leaders. I never really looked or acted the part but we were the ones from our previous form and had been together three years. The bottom streams stayed in their 'clicks' and the middle ones in theirs but we were all as one class."

"The end of the third year came and with it the exams and also my prospect of the top stream, this was the last year for being chosen. I decided to put a good effort in. At the back of my mind was the idea of being put up. But really I thought myself not bright enough for them. I was still taking the anti-depressants as if I stopped the old sickness comes back. It was a whole week of exams and I was trying my best, not for the school, but to put myself to the test to see if I could do it. I hardly ate that week through nerves and indecision. I wanted to come first for my own triumph but dreaded it in case I actually did which meant the top stream. I was terribly mixed up, I didn't know if I was coming or going. The week soon ended. I had managed to do them all except for the last. I had been too exhausted to carry on and didn't think I had a chance anyway. I suppose having thirty-five people above you for three years had smashed my self-confidence. The results came through in the first four subjects, I came first. I was very proud and my self-confidence was restored. But as the following results came I went down and down until the last exam I took I came almost bottom. Perhaps I wasn't all that intelligent after all. I took three weeks to recover. Soon it was time to go back again. I went for three days but now the morning sickness was all day sickness and assembly claustrophobia was school-phobia. For that three days I hardly ate as the more I ate before I went to school the more I was sick when I arrived. I just couldn't go on any longer. I had had enough of the whole system, I had tried my best so I just couldn't go any more. I wanted to a lot as my enthusiasm was untouched, but I was in a terrible rut. We decided to seek professional help. We learned the cure was to break it down slowly bit by bit."

"Not many people understood school-phobia. The psychiatrist did, only what he read in books but hadn't experienced it himself so he wasn't expected to know much. The school did a bit but had only experienced mild cases in the bottom streams, they associated this with laziness. I knew those 'lazy' people, sure they didn't like bookwork much—never did their home-work and were all way off school. But understanding their attitudes, if you looked hard enough, was a mind full of interest." (Valerie continues with reflections on "teacher" attitudes to the lower streams and "less able" pupils.)

"I was going into school now for two hours a day, the school were getting a bit impatient and wanted me back by Christmas two months away ... Soon I shall be back at school full-time, it didn't take me until Xmas like the school wanted, in all it was about nine months before I settled down again."

"Now the 'click' didn't want anything to do with me. I don't blame them as I never told them the real reason for me coming at odd times. As far as they were concerned I had gastro-enteritis, they believed me as I was a stone thinner. It wasn't easy getting back but wasn't impossible like some people thought. Many things made it easier for me. I kept up my reading and would escape from everything into a book but didn't like the shock when I came back to reality. I don't think I would have made it without my best friend, she wasn't in my class but kept me in touch when the 'click' decided to turn their backs on me. I really felt what it was like to be lonely as I always had some school friends. But the fact of attending irregularly made me feel an outcast. My classmates weren't half as bad as I expected, now I sat with a 'click' of girls who were mainly from the bottom stream, they were nice and didn't ask any questions, they weren't bothered with anything . . . I got to see myself as a total rebel doing all the wrong things. But this I thought was a waste of nine months. It was an easy way of getting out of things and the school would be winning that way. I decided to have a complete change. I felt I could face a different school and now felt as if I was getting over an operation and wanted to surge ahead. I must admit in the nine months I was ill I did think about myself a lot but I couldn't go out anywhere. Cinemas reminded me of assembly, anywhere I went where I was locked in, trains, buses, it reminded me of the time I felt sick and trapped. I couldn't even bring myself to look at school books, think of words like assembly, break, school dinners, lines, cane, (not homework, that was done at home), uniform, head-master, head-mistress, toilets (I had spent so much time in them I knew precisely how many toilet rolls, paper towels, bars of soap there were in the place), pen, ink, ruler, chalk, and anything else that reminds me of school. One day all those things will be in a great museum and in its place will be more open plan schools, every school will have a psychologist, and all our schools will be run like a college with greater understanding of schoolchildren. I have already seen some changes. They don't stream pupils until the second year until they know their capabilities. One day our whole educational system will become almost faultless and all our problems will vanish because today's school-children are tomorrow's problems. Drug addicts, drop-outs, violence will be in the giant museum, and I hope one day school-phobia will too. One of the most dis-heartening facts is that you have nothing to show for school-phobia, you look quite normal from the outside but are probably just as miserable as the disabled you see with twisted limbs. Society accepts them for their visual problem but when its inside its far worse."

Valerie's account of herself has been set out here at length, not as a document for diagnosis but as an account of a personal experience. There is practically nothing in the account that relates to home background or to the course taken by those concerned with her treatment. Here, school-phobia is described from the inside and the reader will make his own comments and assessments, but may at least have a better understanding of what it feels like to be a "patient."

A similar self-analysis was printed in the *Journal of the Association of Educational Psychologists* in March, 1973, from a girl of much the same age as Valerie. This shows many points of similarity with Valerie's account.

"I got frightened when I had to go to school. It was as if something out of my control was telling me to run away, not to go to school. I couldn't do anything. It was hopeless. I remember one day describing my fright to myself. It was as if there was a volcano inside me and when I was walking to school its energy would build up and up and as I was entering the gate the volcano would explode. I just had to run away, escape perhaps, and yet why? What was I afraid of? Was it that I was just making excuses for myself and really deep down inside I just didn't want to go? Anyway that was before the summer holidays. It is all in the past. Now I am in the fourth year and it has started again."

Earlier in her account of herself this girl had written of the upsetting effect of parental disharmony and eventual separation. She also writes of her inability to make lasting relationships with her classmates. "In lesson time they would tease me and then the next minute they were really friendly and nice, but I didn't know where I stood with them." The separation of her parents precipitated a condition which had been in existence for at least two years. Truancy, in the sense of the sort of escape to which she referred in the words quoted above, was followed by depression and misery which lead her mother to seek professional treatment. It was suggested that a residential special school would help her, but she did make a great effort and has returned to school with only periodical absences. She concluded her own account of herself:

"Tomorrow I will go to school and will work as hard as I can. The next two years will decide my future. I want a job when I leave so I now know what I am going to do. Start again, turn over a new leaf, whatever you want to call it, this is what I will do. I am one of the lucky ones. It isn't too late for me and I am not going to miss this chance. It will be hard for me but I know it will turn out alright in the end."

Eleven-year-old Tommy suffered a severe attack of school-phobia which was precipitated by the change from primary to secondary school. He was a small, nervous, and rather backward child who had suffered prolonged periods of absence from school for some years. Home circumstances did not offer a very helpful prospect for effective treatment and it was decided to send him to a residential special school. During his first term he described some of his reactions in a sentence completion test of the kind often used in the course of treatment to assist in diagnosis. Some of Tommy's answers are given below, his spelling and writing which are often difficult to decipher, are not reproduced here:

My schoolwork/is all writing.
I hope to become/an actor.

I want to know/how long it will be before I can go home.

I spend most time/sitting down.

What makes me angry is/someone hitting me and smaller boys.

If I/were rich I would donate a lot of money to the old.

I sometimes feel I would like to/die.

My mother/is very kind and has a heart of gold.

In five years time/I hope to be famous.

I sometimes dream/of mum and dad.

There are times/when I get angry.

I sleep/I dream a lot.

My greatest trouble/getting back to school.

Some girls/are pretty.

I cannot understand what makes me/blush.

My father/is a nice person.

I sometimes have pains/in my stomach.

I hate/bullies.

My chief worry/about mum.

I get on best/at home.

The worst time/when I left school.

The news which surprised me most/was that I had to come here.

I am sorry/I am bad (sometimes.)

At home/I do not like getting up.

My temper/is bad.

I get pleasure from/sleep.

I become embarrassed/at girls.

Quarrels are mostly/my fault.

I am ashamed/at spelling and reading.

The saddest day/was the day I came here.

Most of all I wish/I was back at school and I want to be an actor.

The image that children have of themselves is the result

of their own inner feelings, they do not stand away from themselves and make an objective assessment. A child who lacks self-confidence will assume that this is obvious to everyone around him and that they will exploit it. Parents or teachers may try to persuade children by verbal argument that there is nothing amiss with them, that they are as good or as clever as their classmates. But arguments will have no effect against the powerful emotional states which influence both thought and action. The self descriptions and experiences we have referred to are very real to those who suffer them, however unreasonable or even unreal they may seem to those observing them from the outside.

5

The Child and
His Home

IN the previous chapters I have suggested that in many
cases of school-phobia examined by researchers there
appears to be a close association between the anxiety and
depression which characterize these children and the
relationship which they have with their mothers. One
nine-year-old boy said that when he was at school he
knew his mother was thinking and worrying about him
and this made him worried. A thirteen-year-old girl said
that once she discovered that her mother had had problems just like hers she felt much better, and when they
could both discuss their mutual difficulties as equals she
lost much of the anxiety she had felt about school attendance. The mother of a nine-year-old boy was an intelligent and resourceful woman, but had no outlet for her
abilities other than her home where she took the major
role of organizer and administrator. Her husband was by
nature rather a retiring person and became more so as his
wife assumed a male role in family affairs. She, in turn,
felt that her mothering and female role was suppressed
and frustrated. Discussion of her own problems with the
family doctor helped to restore the balance within the
family, bringing a restoration of normality to her son and
a return to proper relationships with her husband.

The family is an intimately related group of individuals, each having a separate set of individual characteristics, attitudes and needs. The husband and wife bring

65

into the family circle their own past as well as their present roles *vis-à-vis* one another. No husband/wife relationship exists purely upon the period of their personal interaction, each was an individual before they met and all that has gone before constitutes a substantial part of their present "life style." The children, on the other hand, stem only from the family to which they belong, apart from the inherited characteristics about which, unfortunately, we know only too little.

The study of the behaviour of any one member of the family can never be pursued in isolation. Each member, of course, exists separately and has his or her relationships outside the family and a personal psychological make-up peculiar to himself, but behaviour is the product of interaction with the environment, and the child's most significant environment is the group of adults with whom he has been brought up from infancy. The most prominent figure in this group is almost certainly his mother. Some children are brought up by people other than their natural mothers, but these are, today, the exception rather than the rule. Some have been reared in institutions from babyhood, and I will deal with them separately, as their circumstances are different, as are the effects. In this chapter I shall look briefly at the ways in which children relate to their parents from infancy, especially to their mothers and what the meaning of this relationship may be for later individual development. But even this close mother/child relationship must not be looked at as though these two members of the family interacted upon one another independently of the father or of other brothers and sisters. The personality of each individual is both his or her own and the family's. The mother is, at the same time, a wife and as such is influenced by her relationship to her husband. The whole group has a life of its own which makes it the sort of family that it is, and in this process each member gives and takes, suffers and profits from this social interchange; the family seeks an equilibrium in its life-style just as does each individual.

An example of the way in which family members interact with one another, sometimes to the cost of each other, is given by the Whistler family who sought advice at a time when, in fact, their own circumstances solved their problem. Mr. Whistler was a successful businessman who had built up his own motor business from scratch and was wholly absorbed in it. He was a good husband and father according to his lights and provided generously for his family. His wife had been a school teacher before their marriage and was an able and efficient woman. In the early years of married life she had acted as her husband's secretary and had been very largely responsible for his success. However, the business prospered, he employed his own secretary and made it clear to his wife that it was now time for her to settle down to raising a family and creating the sort of home that his success merited. This she did and for some years all went well.

Their first child was a boy and he grew up perfectly happily with no troubles at school. The younger child, however, reacted differently. Two years younger than his brother, he found himself alone at home in term time when his nine-year-old brother went to boarding school. Gordon, the younger boy, presented no difficulties in his first two years at school, but his brother's absence precipitated trouble. At first it was thought that this was only a temporary reaction to his older brother's absence, but Gordon persisted with his refusal to return to school, by half-term the mother and father were seriously worried and sought advice. At home Gordon was withdrawn and passive, he suffered bouts of sleeplessness, complained of tummy aches and headaches and although excessively clinging to mother had bursts of apparently unaccountable rudeness and antagonism.

When interviewed, both parents were deeply disturbed

by Gordon's persistent disturbance. Mr. Whistler thought it was basically a matter of discipline and that he should be sent away to board, although he was two years below the age at which his brother had gone. There was probably something in Mr. Whistler's argument but it would have been a flight from the situation rather than a facing of whatever the cause may have been.

Gordon's behaviour did not improve and his mother came for two more discussions with the case-worker, during which she described much of her own personal feelings about the family. A good and able teacher, she had given up her professional career for marriage and then found that her abilities were no longer needed by her husband. She felt frustrated and wasted and concentrated her efforts upon the children. She had more emotional and intellectual energy than could be extended within the family circle. She was often restless and depressed, and her mood was felt acutely by Gordon when he was the only object of her attention. Without him she had no outlet in which to find satisfaction. The case-worker very tentatively suggested that she should find some part-time teaching to provide an outside interest for her energies, but her husband would not hear of this, indeed he thought it would only aggravate Gordon's condition.

Unfortunately for Mr. Whistler, his business suffered a severe set-back, and, to maintain their house and pay school fees, Mrs. Whistler decided to do some teaching. Her husband, under the circumstances, agreed. Within a matter of weeks Gordon very substantially improved. His mother was quite capable of working and running the home, and now that she had an outlet for her energies and felt less frustrated her relationship with Gordon was very much easier. She felt that her work was essential to the family and worthwhile to those she taught; she could release Gordon from the tie which she had sustained with him and he, for his part, no longer had a sense of obligation and dependence towards his mother which his age made it impossible for him to understand or cope with. His mother's new mood of self-fulfilment was reflected in Gordon's revived self-confidence.

So we find in many cases of school-phobia a family situation in which the interaction of the members of the family, together with outside circumstances, can affect the balance of the group as a whole, at one time producing disequilibrium and emotional stress, at another time, restoring equilibrium, sometimes deliberately sometimes by chance.

The attachment of mother and child
Various theories have been put forward to explain the very close relationship that is built up from infancy between a mother and her child. For many years it has been assumed that this relationship is based upon the child's needs for food and warmth. These physiological needs constitute the baby's world and are the goals of his activities; they constitute the difference between comfort, pleasure and pain. It is, therefore, natural to suppose that the one figure in his environment who gratifies these requirements is the one to which he will become attached. In normal circumstances this figure is the child's mother, she feeds and cuddles him, providing him with the warmth and security of her body. What more natural than to suppose that this pleasurable experience is the basis of his love for her and a long lasting attachment to her physical presence?

There are, however, reasons to suggest that this is not entirely so. Man is not by any means unique in exhibiting a powerful relationship between mother and offspring. It is a phenomenon found frequently in the animal world as well. It is from the study of animals that much has been learned that helps us to understand and look afresh at human relationships. Observations of monkeys and apes in both natural and artificial laboratory conditions have taught us much about the way very young primates behave towards their mothers. We have also learnt much about what happens when they are deprived of their natural mother. We have been shown how rhesus monkeys do not select the provider of food when under stress, but take refuge with the flannel "mother," we have seen how baboons develop independence of the mother by associating and playing with young of its own age, and taking refuge with adult males when alarmed. In chimpanzees attachment to the mother persists well into adolescence, and often into adult life. In all the studies it is clear that the mother/child link is maintained by both sides; the baby clings and the mother does not allow it out of sight or retrievable distance. Weaning from attachment to mother is more at the initiative of the young than of the mother, and the age at which separation takes place varies—in some species it is never entirely lost.

From all these observations and experiments we have learnt much about the relationship. It is not by any means confined to the meeting of physiological needs; it is rather a whole range of behaviour patterns in which the young offspring reacts to its environment by maintaining proximity to its mother. In the young human the same sorts of behaviour can be seen as soon as we realize what we are looking for. The proximity of the mother is maintained by both, and much of mother's behaviour is, in fact, dictated by the methods employed by the infant to keep her near him.

This attachment behaviour on both sides persists until the child is around three years of age. About this time an abrupt change is noticeable, and the infant is clearly ready to begin the separation process albeit on his own terms. Security must be assured and he looks for familiarity in the new adults who care for him, he needs to

have known them in company with his mother before he
is fully prepared to surrender himself to them without
her. He must not have cause for fear or feel threatened
by those around him, and he must know where mother is
and be assured of her accessibility. These, briefly, are the
normal circumstances under which a child may be taken
to a playgroup or nursery school shortly after his third
birthday. The new group will constitute the first and
important stage, not of breaking, but of changing the
nature of the attachment to his mother. The personality
of the child will begin to develop through relationships
with his peers and with adults other than those in the
family group. The development of self-confidence will
depend upon the circumstances mentioned which are his
assurances of security.

But though attachment becomes less intense and its
form modified, it remains dominant in the behaviour patterns of the child. The clinging habit of young monkeys,
in which they generally take the initiative, is still apparent
in the four-year-old child and not lost in the school-age
child. Alarm or anxiety, pain or fear, will result in a
quick movement to parent or parent substitute; holding a
familiar hand is a common reaction of children up to the
eve of puberty.

The progress of attachment behaviour should not be
seen as a loss of attachment which culminates in a complete break at some point in adolescence or adult life, but
rather as a continuing relationship far into adult life,
which loses its intensity in terms of physical and
emotional inter-dependence as it deepens in sophistication and recognition of individual roles.

Deprivation of maternal care

It is significant that the majority of children suffering
from school-phobia come from what are ostensibly reasonably good homes. The sort of situations that we normally

associate with deprivation are not common among these cases, indeed many reveal an excessive solicitude on the part of parents. Deprivation, however, is not to be associated solely with separation from mother, although this is its clearest form. There is what researchers in this field have described as "masked deprivation" which covers a very wide range of faulty interaction between child and parent.

Deprived children who have lacked maternal care for a significant part of their infant life may show some of the symptoms which we associate with school-phobia, for example, anxiety and depression. They are often withdrawn and find it hard to make satisfactory contact with either adults or other children; their social development is impaired and they tend to retreat into what seems to be self-sufficiency and self-dependence, shunning interaction with others or interacting inadequately, with aggression or with a degree of self-centredness which makes co-operative play very difficult. Deprived children may also be clinging, but without differentiation as to which adult in their surroundings they approach. They seek out a source of security, but having no consistent attachment figure they seek it out wherever it seems to offer itself; relationships are not consistent or sustained. Though deprivation is evident in the behaviour of truants it is much less evident in children suffering from school-phobia.

Masked deprivation, as its name suggests, differs from overt lack of maternal care in that mother is present throughout the child's infancy and there is no deliberate separation between mother and child. There is, however, a faulty relationship between the two which can take a variety of forms. Much may depend upon the mother's own upbringing, the experiences of her own childhood, and the effect that these experiences may have had upon the development of her own adult personality.

In several cases of school-phobia the child's mother is recorded as suffering from a variety of personality deficiencies. Descriptions of parents as "inadequate," "neurotic," "unstable," as having a disturbed childhood, unhappy childhood, or a sense of failure or frustration in marital relationships, are not by any means uncommon. These characteristics inevitably react upon the quality and kind of mothering that the child receives.

If there are deficiencies in the mother's own personality these deficiencies will be reflected in the child. If the deficiencies are such that the mother lacks self-confidence, is emotionally immature or unstable, then her infant will find stability impossible to discover or achieve. His growth towards self-identification will thus be halted or retarded. He will be constantly and instinctively feeling for something that is not there. His tie to his mother beyond the period at which she should be releasing him to develop on his own will reflect this continuing and unfruitful search. At the same time the mother may well be doing precisely the same thing to her child, trying to find in him qualities that she herself lacks, or trying to use him as a compensation for her own losses as an infant. Much of this, indeed often all of it, may be quite unconscious on the part of a parent who is doing all in her power to provide for her child. It would, therefore, often be both unfair and quite erroneous to attribute blame. It is neither blame nor praise that is needed in the treatment of both child and parent, but understanding and help.

The danger of over-protection

Successful mothering is a delicate and complex operation. It is an immense tribute to human nature that it is normally performed without the need of extensive training or constant correction by the expert. Most mothers do not even know why or how their relationship with their child is what it is; all they know is the depth of their own devotion to the infant and their desire to meet his needs and the pleasure they derive from so doing. It is only at the far ends of normality, at the points of under-caring and over-caring, that the problems that need correction occur. Under-caring is fairly clear in the dangers that it presents and is usually easier to detect and describe than over-care; but the latter can also have dangers.

In the immediate post-natal period of the infant's life the mother/child link is one of identity. The baby's needs are met with an immediacy that reduces any signalling by the infant to a minimum. As time goes on the necessary preoccupation of mother with other duties, however caring she may be, creates a time gap between the infant's sensation of need and the mother's meeting it. It is through this brief period, during which the cries or movements of the infant are signalling need, that self-recognition is able to grow. When hunger is met by immediate presentation of the breast, when the need for warmth and comfort are met by the spontaneous lift and holding of the baby, the capacity to differentiate between his own body and these other objects or sensations of objects, is absent. As soon as he has to cry or gesticulate for them he is beginning to set the scene for a "me and it" recognition. The scene is enlarged as the variability of the object world is borne in upon him by vision and movement. The scene is eventually completed when some of the objects become recognizable as persons and "me and it" becomes "me and you." All the child's senses are employed in this process of awakening to realization of self and to recognition of the chief object of attachment —his mother.

There are other processes through which the child passes in the journey to independence and these have been set out by psychoanalysts in some detail. The anal and oral phases of infant development, whatever attitudes we may adopt towards them, are observable preoccupations of the growing child. But over all there is a process whereby the child and his environment assume an inter-dependence which replaces the complete dependence of the immediate post-natal stage.

But after the infant is a few months old the mother must begin again to be herself; in other words she must begin to assume the separate identity which, of course, she has always had, but which she has temporarily suspended in order to identify with her baby and meet his every need in the early weeks of his life. Her withdrawal from complete identification with him is very necessary to them both. But suppose that she does not resume her own life and remains identified with her child because she fears the step she ought to be taking, because she is excessively anxious about her function in the maternal role. Should this be the case there is always a danger that so close a link will be forged between the two that the separate identity of each will be difficult to establish. They may become emotionally bound together, necessary to each other far beyond the time when interdependence should have become a flourishing independence.

Growing to independence will be discussed in the next chapter when the social aspects of the child's development are considered. For the time being it is important to recognize the need for the mother to wean herself away from too close and protracted a period of identification with the baby, and for this she will need external support. This leads us back to the dynamics of the family group and the realization that no one is isolated in this growth to maturity, but is part of a constantly interacting group of individuals.

The role of father

The chief role of the father in the family is supportive. This he inherits as the traditional function within the pattern of family life in western society. He is the chief source of economic support and as such determines very substantially the material standards that the family sustains. This pattern has undergone considerable modification in the last twenty years as the working mother has become an increasingly accepted part of the social scene. But during the mother's period of child rearing the supportive role remains the primary one.

In the dynamics of family relationships, however, the material provision is subordinate to the emotional stability that can be achieved, and the paternal role becomes complementary to the roles assumed by the other members. Successful families tend to be those in which roles are complementary rather than equal or competitive. It is the "fit" of personalities, rather than their respective strengths, that achieves a harmonious balance between family members.

In case histories of children with school-phobia a very wide range of paternal characteristics are described. Some workers have found fathers who are passive and submissive and have tended to regard this as a contributory factor in the child's behaviour. But many families have fathers who occupy a passive role in connection with their children and many fathers leave a large share of domestic authority and organization in the hands of the mother; such families do not necessarily produce children who refuse to attend school. It is one thing to examine and describe the personality defects of the parents of children with school-phobia, but quite another matter directly to relate these defects to the phobia.

If the fathers of the children are taken in isolation they do not appear to present any defects that are either consistent throughout the group or peculiar to the group. Some defects suggest possible contributory factors to the child's disturbance, but scarcely precise causes. For example, lack of paternal involvement with the children

---

might well result in uncertainty of sex roles and difficulties with adolescent relationships. We also know from research that lack of empathy or affection between father and son may be a feature of delinquent boys. But children found in such situations do not consistently exhibit symptoms of school-phobia. Similarly, the children of broken or abandoned homes do not always figure largely in the groups of case histories that workers have recorded.

Whatever may be the characteristics of individual parents, it is undoubtedly true that the children in a family are subject to the effects of interparental relationships. If there are two or three children who are closely associated by age and circumstances of upbringing these effects will be more thinly spread and more easily borne. But when one child becomes the subject of parental conflict or interaction then the effect upon that one child may be severe. We have seen how over-protection can be the result of frustrated energy or self-justification when other reasons for an unacceptable role seem not to exist.

A child can also be a battleground for the conflicts of his parents, each knowing the guilt felt by the other when the child is hurt or mistreated and so emotionally hitting at the child in order to injure the other partner. Such conduct may be hard to control and is quite beyond the child's capacity to cope with or understand. It produces gross inconsistencies of treatment, as a parent may be loving in compensation for hurt and aggressive in the effort to inflict hurt, not upon the child, but upon the partner. The child is not being recognized or treated as an individual in his own right but as a means to an end. His individuality is thus destroyed and his self-confidence, which is the result of adult acceptance, is unable to grow.

So the father exercises his influence indirectly, rather than directly. The family cannot find the equilibrium it seeks unless all inter-relationships are directed towards the mutual meeting of needs, and the most pressing needs of each member are those that contribute to his or her status as a person with rights and duties which make each both needed by and necessary to the others.

It is beneficial for the child to know that both parents not only want him but need him for their real happiness, but the child is the dependent member of this group and cannot, and should not, have to bear the responsibility of either parent being emotionally dependent upon him. If he is asked to carry this burden it will not be surprising if he exhibits anxiety and signs of stress.

Brothers and sisters

Although a group of children within a family may spread the load of parental interaction, there is no evidence that school refusal is directly associated with only children, or children whose circumstances placed them in an isolated relationship to their parents. Several case histories cited by researchers concern children who have one or more siblings near them in age. In some cases disturbance is shown in different ways by all children in one family, school-phobia being the particular manifestation of disturbance in a particular child.

Relationships between siblings are often fraught with difficulties and animosities, and young children of a family frequently fight among themselves. Jealousy is a very common complaint of children, and not, unfortunately, confined to childhood. In the pre-adolescent stage it is usually associated with the battle for parental attention, and circumstances may often make a particular child the one "left out." These may be circumstances outside the family, anxiety over money or work, change of residence or mother starting work again, and may turn family attention away from a child at the critical stage when he wants it, thus giving the impression of rejection. In times of stress, anxiety or poor health, a parent may use verbal rejection as a defence or threat and it is always the child's interpretation that is important; he believes what he is told and is too young to appreciate the factors bearing upon his parents which make them say what, in fact, they do not mean.

The birth of a baby has been shown in several instances to be a precipitating cause of school-phobia and this is clearly associated with competition for parental attention. Sex differences arouse in young children anxieties about status in relation to one another; young girls may regard themselves as inadequately equipped when they discover that brother has genitals which they seem to lack. Infantile jealousy is a very deeply laid emotion which needs close examination in each case before it can be properly evaluated. The development of the consciousness of sexual roles which occurs in the latency period preceding puberty is a highly sensitive and important time in the emergence of individuality.

6

The Child and
His School

RECENT writers on school-phobia have tended to discount the part played by the school in the causation of school refusal or phobia. Writing about school refusal in a journal of educational research in 1966, Margery Cooper stated that the research so far conducted indicated that the role of the school in school refusal, whether this took the form of school-phobia or of truancy, appeared to be minimal. This judgement should not be taken as definitive, and some writers have pointed out that the causes are very complex and the school may, in some cases, be a part of this complexity. It is very difficult to separate out the factors which are part of the cause and those which are more superficial and precipitate rather than cause the condition of which phobia or truancy are symptoms. Precipitating incidents vary immensely, from incidents at school that the child reports, to more dramatic incidents happening at home such as the death of a pet, a move of house or a family rupture.

Incidents occurring at school are of several sorts, the one most commonly mentioned is behaviour by a teacher which intimidates the child. Quite often such reports, when checked with the school, appear to have little factual foundation. But it is important to try to see the situation as the already disturbed child will have seen it. A quite innocent remark of normal and justifiable criticism, or a raised voice in a moment of quite justifiable impatience, may well be interpreted by the child as a complete breaking down of relationships upon which his tenuous sense of security was based.

But innocuous remarks are not, unfortunately, all to which children are sometimes subjected, and it may be that a teacher's reactions to problems of carelessness or indiscipline are at times quite frightening to children. The power a teacher has in the classroom is absolute, and the child's motive of pleasing teacher is very strong, so that inability to do this can induce considerable disappointment and self-denigration.

There is certainly good reason for accepting at face value the child's own explanations of the causes of his behaviour and then following these through to ascertain the part they are really playing in his anxiety. To reject his attempts to understand himself, however unreasonable the adult may feel that they are, is only to lessen the chances of making a full diagnosis of the case. Many children suffering from school-phobia will simply say "I don't know" to the question "Why do you not want to go to school?" If, on the other hand, they produce explanations that relate to some conflict with the teacher, this suggests that insecurity in adult relationships is a fear which, once brought to light, can be allayed by alerting the teacher to the child's particular need.

If the child's explanations relate to his peers, if, for example, he says "I have no friends," "No one will play with me," "The other children don't like me," then again methods are needed to instil self-confidence in the group situation, perhaps a change to a more protected group or the opportunity of placing the child where his abilities will be above those of the rest of the group, thus attracting group approval. I have mentioned the case of a child whose recovery was effected by putting him for a term in a younger age group where he was able to acquire immediate status by virtue of age and ability, and so gain self-respect and confidence. Once this was established the transition to his own age group was much easier. Such treatment presupposes a considerable degree of flexibility in the management of the school. It also supposes preparedness on the part of the teachers to subordinate organizational convenience to the needs of a particular child, this is not always easy in conditions of overcrowding or large classes, but it can be dealt with provided the overall number of children with problems is proportionately small.

The majority of children enjoy school, but their reasons for this enjoyment are not always those that either parents or teachers would regard as the essential functions of the educational system or the most important reasons for attending school. There is a gap between the roles of the teacher as he perceives them and the motivations of the child. Parents are, generally speaking, more akin to the teacher in their expectations of school than they are to the child. Parents are very concerned with achievement, especially the middle-class parents and those who aspire to middle-class norms of behaviour and status. Teachers are drawn very largely from the middle classes of society and, understandably, they will take pleasure in achievement because it is some measure of their professional competence and success.

The standards that parents expect are very vague. In spite of the efforts of some schools to educate parents in the work and methods of the school, very few parents have any real knowledge of what levels of attainment they should look for in their children or how, in any practical way, they can assess their work. When parents meet teachers on open day at the school they will ask "How is he getting on?" and take the teacher's assessment for granted. In this way they acquiesce in the teacher's self-selected goals because he is the professional person in the school context. If their child is reported as backward, or not exerting the requisite effort, they assume that either the teacher is failing to teach or the child is failing to work, and tend to resent strongly any implication that home is in any way to blame. All this is a natural and desirable state of affairs for the children who are normal in intelligence and behaviour. The teachers want to teach and parents want their children taught. But how do the children see it?

A child's chief pleasure in attending school is primarily social. Whether a child wants to attend school in preference to other possible forms of enjoyable activity will depend upon the intensity of the social integration that he has achieved and the satisfaction it provides. Social play, including games at various stages of sophistication, constitutes a powerful element in the desire to go to school. Success at games adds to this. It is obvious that if social interaction provides motivation for attendance, this motivation will be stronger at schools where there is maximum opportunity for such interaction. Informal group work, with secure but non-authoritarian supervision, may provide such opportunity.

But though enjoyment of social contacts is a strong motivation, others play a part too. Every child's self-esteem is bolstered by success. The opportunity to succeed is sought and enjoyed. The competitive nature of many school situations limits the range of opportunity for success, but acts as a constant stimulus to the more able children. In such an atmosphere the less able child is penalized as he succeeds less often than his more able peers. Furthermore, teachers involved in a competitive system must appear, to the child, to favour the successful and be critical of the less successful. Since "to please teacher" is a primary purpose of every child in the class situation, a continuing inability so to do can be very frustrating.

Most children enjoy learning, and the opportunity

which school offers so to do undoubtedly constitutes good reason for attending. Learning, however, is a complex operation and depends for its enjoyment as much upon method as upon subject matter. From the child's point of view a teacher is there to teach. A good teacher is one who fulfils this very obvious and right expectation. The child wants to learn and appreciates the teacher who enables him to do so. The way in which the teacher achieves this end depends upon his professional skill and judgment, but he knows full well that a balance must constantly be maintained between the pleasure that any method can provide and its success as a learning operation. If he is successful in achieving this balance the child will respond, not only by learning, but by enjoying learning, which is the best tribute that a teacher can receive.

It should not be supposed that enjoyable learning is always associated with informal teaching methods. Children enjoy formal methods provided that they learn from them and so have the satisfaction of achievement. One group of secondary school children so acclaimed a particular teacher that I took the opportunity to watch him at work. In general terms the school was progressive but, owing to its catchment area, had its full share of problems. The children were probably slightly below average in intelligence, and genuine efforts were made to cope with the disadvantaged children. The class in question turned out to be the exception rather than the rule in this particular school. The teacher, who was in his late fifties, was teaching simple and compound interest to second-year children. His methods were the most formal possible: the sums he set on the blackboard were copied and worked by the children, explanations of working methods accompanying each set of examples. In spite of a class of thirty-two children he met every demand for help which was indicated by a raised hand. There was certainly no problem of discipline, and the atmosphere was one of very relaxed and contented business. There was no competition because each child corrected his own work as the examples were worked on the board. No doubt a progressive maths teacher would have found much with which to quarrel in this very formal system, but questions to the children about the lesson brought such replies as "He can really teach he can, even if you are real dumb" and "I reckon its the best lesson of the day for me 'cause I learn something and remember it." There was a clear sense of individual achievement in which the child found real self-satisfaction.

This motivation for school attendance is compounded of the different aspects of school perceived from the child's point of view. The pleasure derived from the natural human instinct for social interaction, the pleasure of learning and acquiring knowledge, the sense of self-satisfaction and the boost to self-esteem from success and achievement, these are the attractive factors which make school attendance worthwhile.

It is not difficult to understand how this whole complex can assume an entirely contrary aspect when the premises upon which it is built are not present in the child's personality. If a child is to enjoy and quite deliberately seek the company of children of his own age in a situation in which choice of companion and membership of a group depends upon his initiative and social adaptability, then he must come to that situation with a reasonable degree of self-confidence. His own personality must be sufficiently integrated, or in the process of integration, to withstand the aggressions and rebuffs from without, as well as coping with the conflicts and frustrations within. If this is not the case his relationships with his fellow pupils will be fraught with so much conscious effort and anxiety that there will be no energy left for enjoyment. The chief motivation for attending school will be no more than an urgent desire within the child which he will constantly declare, continually thwarted by an emotional incapacity to meet it.

This is the underlying problem facing the child who simply cannot bring himself to go to school in spite of his desire to do so. For such a child those times during the day when he is in uncontrolled contact with other children tend to be the most difficult for him to deal with. Many such children find the mid-day school meal particularly difficult. This is a time when, although supervision is given in the general sense, social contact is at its maximum. The anxiety generated by this demand for interaction makes the actual consumption of the meal difficult, and so a vicious circle of mounting anxiety can precipitate the symptoms of school-phobia. The ability to come home for the meal or to have it off the premises and away from the social pressures of the dinner table can often offer some relief and be a help during the period of re-establishment of self-confidence. The same sort of situation can present itself during games periods when membership of a group or team presents comparable pressures on performance.

Learning and the ability to succeed go hand in hand. One must know how to do a piece of work if one is to have a reasonable chance of succeeding at it. It is common knowledge to any teacher that an anxious child or a depressed and worried child will have difficulty in learning. This is not lack of intelligence, it is preoccupation with one problem to an extent that precludes concentration upon another. Children between nine and eleven years of age possess a quite remarkable capacity for a brief but very high level of concentration. This is a natural expression of genuine interest and pleasure taken in a particular task. It is what makes learning worthwhile for children of this age, and is also what makes the teaching of such children so demanding and at the same time enjoyable. But the child who does not have the capacity for this sort of integrated attention is deprived of the pleasure it provides. As he finds learning difficult so he finds achievement equally elusive. In spite of a recognizably high intelligence he will constantly register achievement well below expectation and this will not only make it difficult for him to please teacher, but even more important in his case, difficult to please himself.

The fear of failure in any part of school performance can be a strong contributory factor in school refusal. Children who fail in an ordinary school because of low intelligence or backwardness in basic subjects undergo a similar experience, but it operates the other way round. Self-confidence is undermined by the reiterated accusation of "No good." Failure, of which such children are constantly made aware, often unfortunately by their teachers, more often by their fellows, steadily saps any confidence in their own ability ever to achieve and so eventually they often abandon the attempt altogether. The child who comes to the school situation with the symptoms of school-phobia has little or no self-confidence to begin with and fails for this reason. Indeed he may never manage to bring himself to attempt to succeed, even though he may possess the intellectual capacity to do so with ease.

A further factor is the gap between the environment in which children grow up at home and the environment created by the school which grows out of the aims and ideals set by the staff. The extent of this gap varies according to the nature of the neighbourhood served by the school. In some cases neighbourhood and school match, there is substantial parental involvement and the aims of parents and teachers coincide. In some cases the gap is very wide indeed and the school appears to the child as an alien world expressing completely different values from those to which he is accustomed at home and among the adult and child population of his immediate surroundings. Many writers have drawn attention to this difference of outlook which compels children to live in two worlds, in some cases even to cultivate two languages for use at home and at school. They have speculated upon its effect on the children, its general desirability and how it can be reduced. But it seems likely to remain while most of the teaching staff are drawn from middle-class or white-collar backgrounds and many of the schools in which they teach have preponderantly working-class catchment areas.

This problem is more likely to affect truancy than school-phobia since, as already mentioned, the latter has been shown to affect children of middle-class parents to a much greater extent than the former, and many school-phobia cases come from homes where education is highly regarded.

Although no really hard evidence has been produced to demonstrate the direct connection between the management of the school and truancy or school-phobia among the pupils, much clearly depends upon the school's ability to contain the problem and to some extent deal with it.

The modern primary school, or its equivalents for children up to thirteen, is usually a very flexible educational unit. Modern teaching methods and the development of school design in recent years allow more freedom for the individual child, more emphasis on small groups and individual working and much less formal teaching, except in the basic subjects of reading and number. Children are allowed more opportunity than were their parents for self-expression in many different media, and for the chance to plan their own work schedules and work at their own speeds. Life for the teacher in these circumstances becomes more difficult and demanding, but there is increased opportunity to observe the children and give attention where it is needed. To keep proper records and check the progress of each child is a constant pressure, but if it is managed successfully it does establish a teacher/child contact for each child at regular intervals.

But the advantages of this method must not be allowed to obscure the dangers for the individual child inherent in it. Indeed, the new, open designs of schools, as well as the flexible teaching methods can present a very real threat to the less secure child. The cover for the group provided by the teacher will necessarily be limited by the physical arrangement of the school, and the fact that any one group working at a topic will be supervised directly only part of the time. In contrast, the formal teaching situation provides at least the security of continuous teacher supervision. Even if the class itself is divided into groups it is in one room with the teacher continually present.

In spite of this sort of threat to the security of the child the open situation does seem preferable in many ways. Once the child has been detected by the teacher as in need of special attention, this attention can be given more easily and his problem helped by individual work programmes. This is less practicable in the formal situation in which the whole class may be required to move at the same speed. Furthermore, the flexibility of the open system enables a child to choose his method of working, group or individual, very much as he pleases, his work assignment having been set by the teacher according to his judgment of the child's capacity.

Of course, neither all teachers nor all schools are prepared to operate a fully open and flexible system. There are many different stages between an absolutely formal method and an open one. In very many older school buildings the physical structure determines much of the method, and in modern buildings various compromises in degrees of openness exist. Teachers familiar with one method of teaching are often reluctant to make changes and experiments in situations which are much less clear cut and defined than those in which they trained and practised.

The child's reactions to the school situation may depend very much upon his home environment and his home relationships but it also depends, at the level of personal behaviour and ability to cope with his own problems, upon the pressures which are put upon him to conform to the norms adopted by the school. If these norms are not too demanding, offer flexibility in their application to individual children and also give him some degree of personal choice, then there is a good chance that his reactions will be favourable and his adjustment to school life easier and happier. No school can be expected to relate its organization and methods to the needs of a very small minority of its children. But adaptability and flexibility should form a real part of any educational institution that regards the whole personality of the child as its concern.

7

The Outside World

THE immense importance of the infant's very early stages of development is now generally recognized. Modern research methods and new ways of measuring a child's behaviour have enabled scientists to examine in great detail the gradual development of a child's personality from the very beginning of his life, and to assess the bearing of each stage of this development upon later stages and ultimate adult maturity. Wherever and whenever there appears a break in development, or the normal process has gone awry, it is natural to look back and check the other stages of growth to see whether there were signs there of behaviour which was inappropriate or an environment which did not permit the necessary growth. The development of the human child is a continuous process which must be viewed as a whole, no one stage can be taken in isolation and examined as though it had no antecedent stages from which it had arisen.

When a child needs psychiatric or psychological help it is necessary to know not only as much as possible about the present surroundings of the child, his performance and behaviour but also as much as possible about how he has behaved, and under what circumstances, in the past. Only so can a fair picture be drawn of deficiencies from which he may have suffered, or stages of development which he may not properly have achieved. One stage grows out of another and disorder at one point can produce disorder at subsequent points. This is true of the development of learning as well as of the emotions. If a child has not had the necessary stimulus to learning in his early stages, nor been provided with the appropriate experiences, it may well be that he will experience great difficulty at later stages. One eminent psychologist has worked out, in great detail and with much painstaking research, the order of learning that a child must go through if he is to become numerate, that is, able to handle number and elementary mathematics. If any critical stage of learning is omitted the next stage will not be properly understood.

A similar scheme of development can be detected in the child's growth to independence and the process whereby he is able to separate himself from his attachment to his parent. Just as in learning a child needs to experience certain things in the world outside himself, such as shapes, masses, dimensions, so in his emotional growth to independence he needs certain experiences in relation to the adult world in which he is reared. As discussed in connection with the family, the child's life is a process of interaction, both he and the adult act upon one another, neither side is passive or objective. Growth is achieved by changes in behaviour on both sides which act upon one another to promote a constant process of change that aims, ultimately, at complete independence of functioning. Once independence is achieved the child is able to set about the ordering of his own world of relationships and the controlling of his own emotions and behaviour. He is a person in his own right, able to determine his life in accordance with a developing conscience; the very critical period of adolescence, with its swings from independence to dependence and back again, can be faced with confidence and without the fear and anxiety that result from a distorted or faulty self-image.

The relationship of the child with the world beyond his mother begins very early. It begins, in fact, as soon as the process of integration and self-recognition begins and can be very clearly seen in infants of around six months. Attachment to the mother becomes looser at this period but her presence is, if anything, even more essential than before. Awareness of other human beings, especially strange ones whose presence has not become part of the infant's learned environment, can produce anxiety. If a mother confronts her infant with a strange adult who looks at the child and speaks to him, the chances are that he will turn away and bury his head in his mother's shoulder, from which vantage point of security he will tentatively peep out at the danger presented by this new face. If mother is not present at such a confrontation his anxiety may produce cries or tears. Perceptual familiarity will, however, quickly produce the friendly reaction which is natural to the normal and secure child. If this early stage of extended social contacts is to play its proper part in development it is essential that it takes place from the base of familial security, preferably from the security of the mother's arms.

It is a commonplace in studies of deprived children that harm comes from inconsistent caretaking of a child. A constant succession of strange faces, when no familiarity has been built up from a secure maternal base, can be only a series of traumatic confrontations each bringing its store of anxiety. In time a resistance of indifference is built up, and social relationships produce no responding warmth as the child defends himself by increasing withdrawal from the source of anxiety outside himself.

The introduction to the world beyond the family is therefore a process to be taken carefully and with the supports and safeguards of good mothering; moving from grandparents to aunts and uncles, milkmen, postmen and the people in the local shops, not overtaxing the infant's social capacities but opening up a world of relationships that stimulate interaction and, very soon, communication by touch, holding and conversation. The sensory apparatus of the child moves towards the outside world because it wants to, it is the nature of the human infant and will lead eventually to social play in which the instincts will have the chance to come under control and develop their social constraints and roles.

Play

Apart from feeding and toileting no activity of the child is as important as play. A large number of theories about play have been propounded by psychologists, psychoanalysts and others, but probably no one theory will ever cover the wide variety of uses to which the child puts his play or the many advantages and stimuli to growth and learning that he derives from it. The social advantages of play are only a part of its role in total development, but nevertheless a very important part. As the child grows older play becomes increasingly sophisticated, and its association with moral development arises from the group discipline and rule keeping that it imposes.

For the infant, play is a discovery of the external world and an opportunity to adjust to the limitations that it imposes, but it is also an opportunity to test the strength of self-awareness upon inanimate objects. Play in its early stages is not social but is a preoccupation with self and non-self and a testing of the limits of the growing capacities of the senses of which the child is aware. The most popular playthings for early infancy are those which possess sensory stimulation and which are most pliable: sand, water, dough, paint and so on. These offer no resistance. Toys that require some degree of manipulation and play with other children coincide approximately, since both demand a certain amount of adaptation and so pose a similar problem demanding a similar stage of growth. Children like to play alongside other children at first without the need to interact or communicate. The physical presence of other children will act as a stimulant, a source of imitation for behaviour and play, often as a reason for talking aloud although not necessarily to one another, or at least, not expecting an answer.

Around two and a half to three years of age the child will turn his attention to other children. Their possibilities as play-things rather than play-mates tends at first to inhibit social play; but very quickly, in spite of a strong egoistic element in his attitudes to others, the social instinct predominates and play taken together, even in strife, is preferable to the lone preoccupation with inanimate objects that marked the earlier stage. This period of very early social relationships corresponds to the gradual disentanglement of the child from maternal dependence. If the mother/child attachment has proceeded in the right manner this disentanglement will be sought by both, and the provision of play-groups and nursery schools will fit well into the changing patterns of family life. This first move to independence and extended social contacts is most important and failure to achieve it may impair subsequent attempts at separation. A parent who, for one personal reason or another, cannot allow this separation may be sowing the seeds of many future difficulties.

The encouragement of early social contact must not, however, be so clearly expressed that it amounts to, or appears to the child as, an act of rejection. There is much hesitation, anxiety and unexpressed fear, in the first tentative approaches to social play. This must be recognized and catered for. There should be no sudden dumping of the child on the play-group or unprepared abandonment at a friend's house; least of all should the parent openly belittle the child for his continued attachment to her. All these parental attitudes can be self-defeating, driving the child to seek, all the more fiercely, the love and security that he feels is being snatched from him. The child in the play-group who spends all the session looking anxiously for the returning figure of his mother is a familiar sight to many play supervisors, and the suspicion that mother has made only too clear her joy at leaving the child is the inevitable judgment. Not only do some mothers make their get-away too quickly, but they deliver some such parting shot as "If you don't behave yourself I'll not come back at twelve o'clock." The threat is also used sometimes at home "If you don't do as I tell you I'll leave you with Mrs. Brown [the play leader]." Rejection and over-protection both have dangers at this crucial stage, when tactful handling alone can achieve the transition to new social relations.

The nursery school child who has the opportunity of many social contacts outside the school is undoubtedly at a great advantage over those children between the ages of three and five who have to take whatever home offers. If the transition to the new surroundings is accomplished by just the right amount of release by the mother and acceptance by the school, the child's growth to normal independence is almost assured. But it is again the total family situation that can determine success or presage trouble at the later school stages. The embracing security of home is replaced by another type of security. The nursery school is an enclosed world and teacher/child relationships are close, groups are kept small compared with those of primary school, emphasis is upon controlled and carefully selected play, much of the aim of the nursery school is satisfactory socialization and the child's progress in this, or difficulties encountered on the way, are observed and managed by the teacher. Emergence from nursery class to the infant department of primary or first school is another step into a new sort of world.

In the two years immediately preceding primary school, the critical process of gaining personal identification and discovering the limits of personal freedom causes immense emotional turmoil in the young child. He wants

98

both freedom and security at the same time. He must continue to rely absolutely upon his parents, but equally he must have the opportunity to rebel against their restraints. It is not unusual for children at this period to be rude, destructive and defiant. Some parents find this distressing and react either with anger or evident anxiety. In all probability anger is the better choice, if it must be one or the other, it is an emotion the child can understand and react to, anxiety will only transmit itself to the child and build up guilt which will be a nagging impediment to his search for freedom. The need, during this difficult period, is for consistent discipline and tolerance, the maintenance of order and the continuing acceptance of the child's person in love and security, as well as making disapproval of socially unacceptable behaviour quite clear to him. The child wants to produce a reaction and there should be one, but not of a sort that will bring into question the sense of security in which he may exercise his rebelliousness. Thus the reactions of parent and nursery teacher or play leader should coincide and the two worlds prove consistent in the learning to which he is being subjected.

Play at this stage becomes of great significance. It is a medium for social interaction as well as a means of solving some of the emotional conflicts and puzzles that the child faces. The normal child will use his playthings as substitutes for the less pliable situations and persons which form the real world. He will use fantasy to solve otherwise insoluble mysteries of adult behaviour, and relieve his pent-up feelings of love and hate upon inanimate objects over which he has complete mastery. Many children have a link between fantasy and reality through a pet object, often a piece of rag, an old vest, which is taken everywhere, held, sucked and cuddled. It is a link between the world of inner fantasy and the outside world from which it has been taken. Such objects must be treated with respect, and when the child naturally, and of his own free will, discards it a new stage will have been begun and an old one left behind.

It is interesting to note that in several cases of school-phobia, both early and around puberty, parents report that their children are not playing with their toys although many, probably far too many, were provided. Clinicians report the same behaviour in school-phobia cases placed in their play therapy rooms for observation. This might well suggest that, for some reason, these children have been unable to play, and so lost the therapeutic outlet it provides.

Facing the school situation at five is both exciting and distressing. If all is well, and the pre-school period has had preparatory social interactions built into it, the excitement of the new environment will over-ride the distress that separation from the security of home and mother may cause. But just as the child is facing a new environment and welcoming the stimulation it provides in new experiences and new relationships, the mother is facing a new child and the necessity of adjusting herself to a fresh role. This adjustment may not come easily. At one level of her consciousness she is delighted that her child is growing up and is part of the wider social life of school, just like the children of her friends and neighbours. She wants him to be normal, independent and to have friends beyond the limits of home. At another level she resents his independence, her own role in relation to him, to the home and to her husband is threatened by the removal of the child who so adequately justified her existence as wife and mother. Her love for him which aroused and sustained her maternal instincts is now being asked to release him so that he may make other attachments. The great majority of mothers adjust perfectly satisfactorily to this demand by taking up relationships, friendships and activities that had been curtailed during the early years of the child's life, or there may be a younger child still at home to fill the gap. Some mothers, however, find this a difficult period. They may become depressed or anxious without really knowing why and this can easily transfer to the child, who will feel that this daily departure from home causes suffering to his mother. The essentially reliable and secure nature of home as a place to come back to is impaired, and school may become a threat to his security as well as being a stimulus to his independence and social interests. Although most consultants concerned with school refusal find themselves dealing with children in the early years of puberty, some record instances as early as five and six and associate these with the inability of the family to adjust to the new situation of school, or with internal family relationships which are brought into the open by the child's reaction to school. In such cases there has probably been a steady build-up towards a situation which school precipitates, since it represents the demands of the outside world to which the child must, but cannot, adapt.

The relationship of child to teacher is of considerable importance in these early months of primary school attendance, and is a very real reason for maintaining the pressure on school authorities to keep the size of infant classes low. Unfortunately it is often the learning situation which is used as the reason for pleading for smaller classes. In fact research suggests that if the teaching methods are right the learning need not suffer, but undoubtedly socialization does. Not only is it difficult for the teacher to let the attachments form, but inter-child relationships tend to go unsupervised and the sense of security that the reception class should foster is made much more difficult.

Social development during the junior school period of the child's life, that is from seven to eleven, centres round two areas of experience. First there is the need to integrate with his peer group and then to extend his knowledge of the world about him by individual and group discovery. The five-year-old is still in need of an embracing security which follows from home to school with close personal ties that make separation from mother tolerable. The seven-year-old is much freer to accept the ever widening stimuli which crowd upon him as the degree of security that he requires diminishes in intensity. The release that should have developed with the beginning of school enables his physical energy to be directed outwards, both to his peer group and to his environment.

Integration into a group of children of his own age demands that the child shall himself be well on the way to personal integration. In the school or junior club situation it is possible for adult leadership to establish a general covering of security, so that the group may take its time to become inter-related and work or play as a unit. This sort of supervision will provide for the less integrated members to acquire that degree of independence which enables them to direct their attention away from themselves. But in the normal unsupervised groupings of the playground or neighbourhood this covering is only partial or even non-existent and the small gang can be a severe threat to the child who lacks self-confidence.

This is a period of emotional consolidation when the child's inner life is stabilizing and receiving influences and experiences from without. Adults and older children are powerful exemplars, hero-worship and an attraction towards cultural types appealing to the young will produce a wide range of enthusiasms and interests. Friendships are important but transitory, and parents a source of supplies and facilities rather than demonstrable affection. But there remains, as there will right through adolescence, the need for a secure and stable background, although it seldom seems to receive overt recognition.

It is during this period that children become aware of sex differences and sex roles. Identification with the parent of the same sex takes place early, around the age of four for boys and even earlier for girls, but the conscious modelling of the self on parent or other adult is a part of the resolution of individual personality as the child grows towards puberty, by which time consciousness of the sexual role needs to be firmly established. If for some reason this does not take place the sense of personal identification is impaired and self-confidence in the face of the child's peer group is undermined. Children who are uncertain of their role will often exhibit exaggerated defence behaviour. Girls will fuss unduly about dress, toileting and make-up, reassuring both themselves and others that they are indeed girls. Boys are afraid of appearing girlish, of being teased for effeminate appearance or behaviour, and will boast of their association with girls or fantasized manly behaviour. These are, of course, forms of behaviour familiar enough in children around the puberal stage of development, but when coupled with evident anxiety may be signs of disturbance. School refusal is frequently associated with somatic pains, abdominal or respiratory, and these symptoms may be associated with anxiety about sex role.

The whole problem of the determination of sex role in children is a complex one, and accounts in many instances for the outbursts of ambivalent behaviour and personal uncertainty that is so typical of adolescence. Many psycho-analysts base their work on the Freudian theories surrounding the Oedipus complex and its resolution in eventual identification with the parent of the same sex, mediated by the subconscious sexual attachment to the parent of opposite sex. Some psychologists reject this theory, regarding it as theory only, and having little or no basis in empirical evidence. Nevertheless it does suggest underlying causes of disturbances that are associated with the emergence of sexual consciousness.

A child's relationships with his peer group are of

immense significance to him. From puberty right through adolescence they are the focus of his emotional life. But behind these relationships he needs to be able to distinguish the security of the family setting. This security must be able to bear, not only his concept of himself, but also the powerful forces of hate, love and rebelliousness which he must work through in order to control and integrate them. Between the family and the outside world there must be not a gulf but a bridge which is built up brick by brick by the continual adaptations which the child's human environment makes to his changing needs from baby to mature adult.

8

Parents' Dilemma

NINE-YEAR-OLD Desmond had been attending an independent boarding school as a weekly boarder for a term and a half. The school was twelve miles from home. For his first year he had been a day boy and though work was a little hard as he had previously attended a county primary school with a different curriculum, all had gone quite smoothly. It was at his own request that he boarded and he seemed to enjoy his first term. During the first half of the second term there was a marked reluctance to return to school after the weekends. But this did not seem to be significant and his parents did not take it very seriously. The real trouble came after the half-term break when he flatly refused to go back.

He was taken to school by car by his mother. Some tearful protests before setting off were dealt with firmly. But on arrival nothing would persuade him to leave the car. He kicked, screamed and clung to the steering wheel. Neither persuasion nor threats were effective and his mother brought him home. Once home he slowly reverted to normality. This process was repeated three successive mornings after which his mother gave up, and sought advice from the head-master and a psychiatrist of her acquaintance. The school staff were worried and upset by the occurrence and did all they could to help. This behaviour did not appear to be caused by Desmond's school relationships either with his classmates or the staff. Indeed, Desmond himself made no complaints about school, and the school reported no apparent problems in relationships between Desmond and the other children. This was the beginning of a prolonged period of school-phobia which took a year and a change of school to resolve.

What should or could his mother have done in the event of so apparently sudden an onset of disturbance? In the first place the importance of early detection cannot be over emphasized.

For very many children school is a happy and enjoyable experience, made so by the skill of staff and the growing child's natural bent towards social activity. But for some it is a trial to be borne and a set of pressures to be withstood. A continuing reluctance to attend school after the first few weeks of attendance is a symptom of the child's sense of being under pressure. The pressure may be no more than a dislike of certain school activities, of antipathies with staff or other children, and even if it does not wear off after a reasonable time it may be well within the child's competence to manage. No child should be so shielded from pressure that he never learns to withstand it. The sensitive parent on the other hand, with an eye to the future development of the child as well as to his present well-being, should look closely at these symptoms and assess the degree of distress that is suffered. If a child is withdrawn, finds it difficult to play or sleep, then it is unwise to dismiss it out of hand as a natural reaction of childhood. We are tempted to do this as parents simply because we are afraid of disturbance in our children. There is also the deep fear that a child of ours who "goes wrong" is a sign of our failure as a parent.

Parents find it very hard to admit to bad parenting, yet no parent is perfect and every child represents a new challenge and a new responsibility. There are few, if any, infallible guides on how to bring up children. It is one thing to know how to feed them and toilet them and keep them physically well, but that having been achieved all that we ourselves have been and are is brought to play upon our care for them. Much of what we do, the mistakes we make, indeed the mess we may make of it, often stems from our own long standing defects, which the years have made it difficult to remedy.

If we are to be reasonably successful parents it is worth starting by being prepared to look realistically at our own condition. By the time we reach the age of parenthood it is bound to be a mixed condition, and much of what we have learned to accept for ourselves and rationalized as justifiable in our own circumstances may not, by any means, be acceptable to our children.

If, therefore, a child appears to show signs of strain the reason may lie within his own home, within his own personality which has not managed to adjust itself to the particular patterns of behaviour and relationships by which he is surrounded.

It is very difficult for parents to look objectively at themselves and at their own relationships, particularly if the need is to do so critically and without sparing their own feelings and their sense of guilt. Such an effort is more likely to produce cross accusations between husband and wife than calm admissions of fault or failure. Such recriminations will only further exacerbate the child's condition and make him more anxious. The course most likely to produce results is the consultation with a third person who can stand outside the situation and, with both sympathy and expertise, help and advise. The only person really qualified for this role is the family doctor. In all the literature of school refusal the family doctor stands out as the key person in the early detection of emotional disturbance. Even if he himself is reluctant to advise, from either a sense of inexperience in this field or lack of time to enter upon what may be a prolonged process, he is far the best person to recommend another source of help.

Furthermore, in cases in which the child's condition has

107

not yet reached the dramatic behaviour that Desmond displayed, but is yet sufficiently worrying to cause the parents some self-searching, the family doctor is really the only person who can be consulted without the parents appearing to be fretting unduly about something that has not yet demanded educational or psychiatric attention.

First then, the family doctor at the stage at which preventive action may be possible. But at the same time school itself, which is the crucial point of disturbance, must not be left out. The majority of head teachers are aware of the problems of school refusal and are sensitive to the needs of individual children for whom school is a source of anxiety. They are also only too aware of the lack of parental contact in cases of children who present problems of behaviour or discipline. They are glad to see parents and to discuss frankly the difficulties and anxieties that they have about their children.

Many parents are half-afraid of their children's schools. This may be due to a residue of awe and fear remaining from their own schooldays; it may also reflect something of the "us and them" feeling that people have about institutions that seem large, forbidding, and professional in the sense that you cannot argue with them because they have all the answers. These are very largely subjective attitudes. Some schools are large and forbidding, and confuse the outsider who does not know his way about the building or how to gain access to the people he wants to see. It cannot, unfortunately, be denied that there are head teachers and other members of the profession who will say in so many words "I know best what is good for your child, you are only his mother." But such teachers are now few and far between and most are only too pleased to meet parents and involve them in some activity of school life. Parental preparedness to become so involved will be a great step forward in the process of prevention. Research has demonstrated, with a mounting volume of evidence, that parental interest in school life, school work and personal contact with staff has a tremendous effect upon the child's achievement, both social and academic. There is a sense of the unity of the world in which he lives which overcomes the "double life" and double standard feeling that is given by the complete separateness of home and school, the conflicts and stresses of each will be partly carried by the other and the efforts of both will be directed towards the best interests of the child.

In Desmond's case certain family circumstances militated against effective preventive action. Subsequent discussion with both the child and his parents elicited evidence of a certain amount of past difficulty in school attendance. But, due to the sympathy of the staff at his primary school, he had eventually settled there for two very happy years. To him it was the best school in the world. Then came a move, and the decision to send him to an independent school. This decision was supported by the relative inadequacy of the local village school, and the feeling that as his brothers and sisters had attended independent schools with success he should be given the same opportunity. He withstood the change for a whole year in spite of the new pressures of work, but the effort was too much when he became a weekly boarder, a term and a half precipitated the crisis. From the family side both parents were in new professional posts which demanded time and attention. Desmond's old school and friends were more than a hundred miles away, his preparedness to board fitted the commitments of the parents and its dangers were overlooked because of the advantages that it offered. Desmond was the fourth child of the family and separated from the other children by several years, he was therefore virtually the only child of middle-aged parents. By the time he reached school age family patterns were too inflexible, attitudes too established for danger signals to be heeded. When the blow fell all were equally at sea.

What useful steps can be taken when a crisis has been reached and no previous warning has been recognized or heeded? Firstly, the sense of confusion and shock, at what can well be a disturbing situation, must be reduced by recognizing that neither the child nor his behaviour are unique and that others have undergone the same sort of experience. Help is available and in spite of the sense of personal affront that this particular occurrence may cause there is no need for desperation or anger. The child's behaviour will be alleviated if he is allowed to remain at home, so lifting the pressures of school attendance.

Whether or not the aim should be as immediate a return to school as possible will vary from case to case, and should not be assumed to be the most desirable course. It may result in repeated traumatic behaviour at the school entrance or at home before leaving the house. It may deepen the child's depression or anxiety and make subsequent treatment more difficult. The theory underlying immediate return is simply that the child must be made to face his fears and to protect him from them by allowing him to stay away will only make the eventual return more difficult. But this is arguable, and compromises are often better than the sort of confrontation that forcing a return may cause.

I have already discussed the benefits of helping children avoid the anxiety-making occasions, to come home for lunch, to miss assembly, to come home on games afternoons, to be allowed to work in the head's study or the library instead of doing P.E. In order to make such compromises possible two things are necessary: first to get the child himself to say what particular thing(s) he most dislikes and then to gain the co-operation of the head teacher. This is where the family doctor can frequently be helpful. Children will often repeat their denial that anything is wrong at school and just say they do not know why they cannot go. But if a third person not directly associated with the emotional stresses that the situation has generated, can be allowed to gain the child's confidence, useful guide-lines can be obtained and a compromise arranged. Once calm is established and the child feels that someone is listening sympathetically to him and taking him seriously, he will then be better able to talk about himself.

Desmond's return began slowly. He was met at lunch-time by his mother and taken out to lunch and he was also allowed to miss games. Both were times of confrontation with his classmates and this he feared, though by all reports from the school, quite unnecessarily. However, he said he was willing to return on this basis. Once his explanation was accepted and acted upon he began a partial return and his anxiety lessened.

The real issue is force or persuasion. It seems more reasonable to suppose that a voluntary return under any circumstances is preferable to forceful methods with their accompanying struggles, crying and vomiting. Knowing, as we almost certainly do, that school-phobia is associated with the relationship to mother, she is the most likely person to be the active partner in whatever arrangements are made. But if this is impossible then means should be found at least to avoid the points of greatest stress that arise during the school day. One boy of nine who was forced to return to school, in spite of his protests, because his mother had to go to work, found his own solution by making friends with the school caretaker. A little worried about him, the caretaker had a word with the head-mistress. She recognized and explained Stephen's trouble, and asked that he be allowed the privacy of the boiler room for lunch if he wanted it. The caretaker agreed and took over Stephen in lunch periods for half a term, often taking him home with him or giving him little jobs to do in which Stephen took great pride. Stephen acquired a real interest in the school building and a knowledge of it from the caretaker's standpoint that was far more detailed than that of his classmates. He actually looked forward to school, expressing real concern about maintenance work done during the holidays. School is a community, and children may often profit from realizing that it has ramifications beyond the classroom that they may at times regard with anxiety or fear.

School attendance, however it is achieved, only solves part of the problem. School-phobia is an intense emotional disturbance of which refusal to attend school is the overt expression. There is always the danger of thinking that once a child has been persuaded by force or compromise to go back to school the problem has been solved and normality restored. But unfortunately this is not by any means certain, and the expression of his disturbance may well issue in some other form now or later. His return is welcome as it shows some mastery of his own fears, but if a cure is to be effected some treatment should accompany the return, and the referral of the child to a psychiatrist is a wise and necessary precaution. In the process of treatment that follows the co-operation of the parents is essential and will almost certainly be required by the psychiatrist. Frankness, the recognition of the need for outside help and advice, and the need to make any sense of guilt or shame productive in the child's interest, instead of a barrier to his treatment, are as necessary to a period of psychiatric treatment as they would to a consultation with the family doctor. Before the psychiatrist agrees to offer treatment the family doctor will be consulted and there will therefore be a double opportunity for discussion.

A child who is away from school for a prolonged period is, of course, missing tuition which may be very important. Parents are naturally anxious about their children's school performance, but this must be kept in proportion. Except at critical periods, such as the term preceding "O" or "A" level exams, it is doubtful whether putting pressure upon a child to work at home will really be worthwhile, as pressure usually adds to anxiety. If, however, the child is willing to read or work at home or in the local library, this should be encouraged. This may sound like a statement of the obvious, but in fact quite an important decision has to be taken in regard to work during a period of school-phobia. As Valerie recorded in the account of her feelings, quoted in Chapter 4, things associated with school can increase the sense of anxiety and frustration. This is just what, at this juncture in the child's disturbance, we do not want to do. On the other hand, some continuance of work may be part of the compromise arrangements for a return to school. Some children have no real objections to the work and will accept the directions of their teacher if they can do what is set them in some degree of privacy.

In cases of prolonged absence home tuition may be available for children who are under treatment and whose absence is at the recommendation of the psychiatrist or family doctor. Application for such facilities may be made through the school, or information obtained by writing directly to the local education department. Certainly help should be obtained to keep the child used to some pattern of work, and the head teacher will often be the person best able to advise.

When a child is undergoing treatment, the educational psychologist and the educational welfare officer may both have some contact with parents and may certainly be consulted at any time by making a request to the head teacher. If the child has been referred to the child guidance clinic, the clinic social worker will be a most valuable source of help both before treatment begins and while it is in progress. It will be through the social worker that the psychiatrist will suggest how the parents may best be able to help their child towards recovery and a return to school. Some of the advice that he gives may require considerable family adjustments, such as the temporary relinquishment of employment by the mother, or the modification of her working time. He may suggest routines for the child which conflict with the normal family ones, or he may even suggest the removal of the child from home altogether. In all these circumstances discussion and help with the arrangements to be made are part of the social worker's function.

Sending a child away from home may sometimes be necessary, and if it is recommended it will be for a very good reason. Parents may feel that it is a direct assault upon their capacity to manage their own child, but what we have learned of school-phobia shows that what the child may need above all else is to manage himself and grow in independence. Parents also may need to learn that they have a life of their own as well as that which revolves around their child, they too may need to recover their roles as independent people. A period of separation does not mean a complete severance of relationships, nor is it an accusation of guilt or failure, it is a constructive step to resolve what has become a situation from which neither parent nor child can make a step forward. Mutual love is not diminished, nor is the family broken, but a new way of living is initiated from which all may profit if it is used without a sense of guilt or desperation. And all parents of school-phobic children must remember that theirs is not an isolated case, it has happened before, it will happen again, and even as they are struggling to re-solve the problem for themselves and their child, so are very many other parents all over the country.

9

Problems of Treatment

ANY attempt to treat a child who cannot attend school presupposes a diagnosis which places him in one category or another of school refusers. It is this process of diagnosis which raises many questions about the child, his family and the parts to be played in his problem by the various agencies which are individually or jointly concerned with treatment.

It has already been pointed out that the line between truancy and school-phobia is not always a straightforward one. It is fairly easy to draw up a list of the symptoms of school-phobia after an examination of a number of clear cut cases, but this is in fact a process which follows diagnosis, rather than diagnosis itself. Many of the children who do not attend school do not necessarily exhibit these symptoms to the people who are dealing with them. Everything turns upon the degree of interest that parents have in their child, or the time they have to give to his problems. The most blatant exhibition of "phobia" appears at the moment of actually entering school itself. If a child suffering from school-phobia can relatively easily avoid this moment his symptom may not show itself. Anxiety or depression may possibly be missed by inattentive parents, or be attributed to other causes. As one mother remarked "She'd just begun her periods and I thought that was why she was acting funny." She may have been partially right, but it was a very small part of the whole problem. Another mother blamed exams and again was partially right, in that this particular pressure probably brought her son's anxiety to a breaking point. Both these mothers had, in fact, regarded their children's secret truancy as disciplinary problems which could be dealt with by threats and a firm hand, only when their children showed more distinct behaviour troubles did it occur to them that something really was wrong. The first child refused to put on school uniform and would not have any part of the uniform visible in her room; the second eventually refused to leave the house in the morning, and the symptoms usually displayed at the school entrance took place at the front door. Both cases had been regarded, for four years in the case of the girl and two in the case of the boy, as wilful truancy, for the most part without parental knowledge.

The girl's case illustrates some of the difficulties posed for those who are trying to help, as well as for the children concerned. Olive came to the notice of the child guidance clinic when she was thirteen years old. She was brought by her mother on the advice of the head teacher of her school. Olive's attitude to school, school uniform and even her school books was something which her mother could not disregard and she had a tearful and, for her, difficult interview with the deputy head of Olive's school. The head, on hearing such details as his deputy had been able to elicit, arranged an interview with the psychiatrist. Diagnosis at this stage in simple terms of school-phobia requiring treatment was straightforward, but eliciting a detailed case history was more difficult. Olive's mother was clearly aware that she had not given her daughter's anxiety and unhappiness anything like enough serious attention. She, therefore, felt guilty and was reluctant to open up. Several prolonged and tactful home visits by an experienced social worker slowly brought out the facts. Olive herself, both verbally and quite articulately on paper, was anxious to explain her own feelings. For the first time in four years she felt her frequently suppressed problems could be brought into the open and laid before a sympathetic listener. Her difficulties over school attendance had begun when she was nine. There had been absences both with and without her mother's knowledge. She had been helped by her only confidant, a friend who lived close by, who had often made excuses for her at school. At the critical time of changing from primary to secondary school, Olive's parents moved house and she could no longer go to school with her friend, although she met her once they were there. Olive's "truancy" became more persistent and the head teacher complained to the parents who treated it as a discipline problem. On one occasion the educational welfare officer called but, because mother was able to produce adequate excuses, which she was anxious to do, and Olive managed to get back to school, nothing further was done. What appeared to precipitate Olive's final refusal was the discovery that her friend enjoyed the company of some of the boys at school, walked home with them, and no longer bothered to give time and trouble to Olive and her problems. Thus abandoned she gave up the struggle and refused to go at all.

From Olive's side a lot of small details emerged which together confirmed the diagnosis. She had dreaded school meals from the very beginning, and would often leave the building immediately after the last period of the morning and come back just as afternoon school was starting. She could not join in playground activities and would avoid these by prolonged visits to the toilet. She suffered from stomach pains and headaches and would ask to be allowed to sit in the library alone. She would plead sickness and ask to go home; on these occasions her friend would undertake to see her home and it appeared that on a few such journeys she went to the park instead, knowing that there was no one at home anyway. However, over the whole period Olive had achieved a lot. There were times when, as she put it "I really did manage to make it for quite a long time." Her friend was a great help, but the outcome was an anxious, depressed and unhappy child whose mother should have sought professional help very much earlier.

Treatment consisted of weekly visits to the clinic and similar weekly visits by the clinic social worker to the home. For the remainder of the term Olive agreed to attend school in the afternoons only. Her mother was persuaded to do part-time work instead of full time at the local supermarket; the social worker arranged this with the personnel officer of the store, and though reluctant, mother agreed. Olive was desperate to discuss her feelings and sought urgently for explanations and causes. Slowly this urgency and self-obsession wore itself out and helped by some mild anti-depressant drugs, the depression and unhappiness lifted. School, clinic and home cooperated, and by the end of a year Olive was attending school regularly and happily.

During the course of Olive's treatment a certain amount of her early childhood emerged, but though the causes probably lay there it helped her to come to terms with herself, rather than provide an academic diagnosis of her condition. The most elusive person in the whole case was Olive's father who was a long distance lorry driver. He was at home very little, and although he provided generously for the family he took little part in its economy or its social life. Here perhaps lay a major factor in Olive's relationship difficulties. It could almost be said that Olive treated herself, once she had an adult audience of patient listeners.

I have dealt at length with Olive's case because it illustrates well some of the difficulties of detection and treatment. At any time during the four years Olive could have been classified as a truant and dealt with as simply a discipline problem. As an intelligent child she coped with her problem alone, produced the right excuses and kept out of trouble. Indeed the headmistress of her primary school remembered her as "a rather lonely child, inclined to play truant at times, but intelligent and did not give any trouble."

The case also raises the question of who is to be treated. All that has been said about school-phobia and truancy draws attention constantly to the environment in which the child has been reared. No doubt there is good reason to suggest that genetic factors cannot be disregarded. School is an atmosphere of noise and movement and also of enclosure. Cases have been cited in which each of these factors can have a severe physical effect upon certain children. Five-year-old Susan was placed in the reception group of a progressive private school which had elaborate apparatus and a high staff/child ratio. For the first few days she played happily and excitedly with the things put in front of her. After two weeks a member of staff noticed that from time to time she would withdraw to one side of the room with her hands over her ears. Subsequently she refused to go into the room at all, and would block up her ears on entering the school and struggle to get out.

Tyerman cites the case of a girl who felt oppressed inside the school building and felt better when allowed to get out into the fresh air. These attacks of claustrophobia coincided with her menstrual periods and were associated with fear of death. When she was assured of the freedom to leave the classroom when she wanted to and had a chance to talk over her fears she was able to attend school happily.

Intelligence is partly a hereditary matter, though the precise association between intelligence and genetic factors is difficult to establish. In so far as low intelligence may be inherited, it is clear that poor school performance may have a genetic origin. Since most truants appear to be of low intelligence the genetic factor in truancy cannot be neglected. But when all these considerations are given due weight so far as we are able to assess them, it is still true that family relationships loom very large in school-phobia cases and general environmental factors in truancy.

Treatment therefore must be widely based. It cannot be confined solely to the child unless diagnosis is so clear and specific that other factors can be safely omitted. This may be the case with older children who are capable of articulating their problems and can so be helped to work through them. But the younger the child the more necessary it becomes to extend the treatment to the mother. Writing of the treatment of very young children from the point of view of a general practitioner, Clyne records cases in which the mother made very clear her consciousness of her own part in the child's school refusal. On occasion he believed it possible that the mother could be treated alone, but generally mother and child together were seen and their mutual problem opened up.

Father appears remarkably little in the literature on school-phobia. This is mainly because investigators have placed most weight in diagnosis upon the mother/child relationship. Yet frequently workers become aware that the mother's dependence upon the child is the result of an unsatisfactory or unfulfilling relationship with the father. Similarly, cases arise of the child's sex role development being deficient because of a strong mother and weak father situation in the family group. Clyne found considerable variety among the personalities of the fathers whom he met, and was not prepared to attribute causes to personalities. But clearly family dynamics demand consideration of the total unit, and treatment of one parent and the child will be liable to miss vital points in the relationships of the whole group.

All this points to the importance of the function of the

social workers attached to the psychiatric services. It also emphasizes the point made by Clyne that treatment by the general practitioner has the great advantage that he is assumed from the start to be concerned with the whole family. Furthermore, his professional skills enable him to cast his treatment very wide in terms of the complaints from which the family may suffer individually or collectively. He is competent to diagnose and assess supposed illnesses in child or parent, decide the degree of objective reality of the illness, its possible cause and the degree to which it is a cause or effect of the school refusal of the child. Of course on the other side is the parental conception of the doctor's role in family problems. It is unfortunately true of recent years that the ordinary citizen's idea of the doctor as a family confidant in a wide variety of problems has tended to narrow itself to that of a dispenser of prescriptions for specific and recognizable illnesses. Many parents would not associate the doctor's role with problems of school attendance unless these were accompanied by very obvious somatic complaints which required medical treatment. People tend to divide up into clear compartments the sort of help that they consider they need, according to the several helping agencies that are available. "This is a school problem," "This is a doctor problem," "This is a social services problem," "For this I go to social security" and so on. Frequently their assessments are faulty and they miss opportunities of help that might otherwise have been given them. This is a difficult problem to solve, particularly as within any one of the possible agencies there are several possibilities, as discussed in Chapter 10, and there is no absolute guarantee that the right one will be chosen. On the doctor's side there is also the growing pressure of work and the extent to which he is able or willing to accept cases for treatment which go beyond his medical terms of reference. He may, quite justifiably, feel that other agencies exist for this purpose.

Aims and methods of treatment

In discussing aims of treatment a distinction must be made between the presenting symptom—inability to go to school—and the underlying development or relational problem. Those concerned with treatment must make a decision about what they propose to treat since treatment of both these factors simultaneously may be contradictory. An early return to school is, of course, superficially what everybody, including the child, wants. But if the return is to be of any real value, it must be a return on the right terms. There are compromises such as those already cited, of partial return, going back home during the lunch hour, returning to a lower form with less pressures and so on. These may be effective and help growth to maturity by allowing a certain degree of regression to an earlier starting point. But enforced return may be counter-productive and simply suppress symptoms that will recur when a subsequent situation reactivates them.

Clyne has summarized very well the real aims of treatment as "the re-establishment of the relationship function at a development level appropriate to his age." He admits that this is a very wide aim and covers a multitude of contingent aims among which return to school is one. But the advantage of the definition is that it throws the weight of treatment upon the full restoration of the child's personal development. It is a child-centred aim rather than a society-centred one. When first discussing school-phobia I drew attention to the social pressures upon both child and parents to conform to behavioural norms, of which school attendance is one. The danger of such pressures is that they may inhibit the right treatment of the child in favour of mere conformity. There is also a danger of excessive professional self-confidence among teachers which prompts some to assume that if the child can only be got back into their control they can wave the magic wand that will effect a complete cure. This is not the attitude of all teachers by any means, nor is it confined to the teaching profession, but it is a vocal opinion against which those concerned with treatment must be on their guard.

The transfer of the child to another school is a natural reaction of parents who, when first presented with the child's behaviour, will attribute the fault to the school he currently attends. The child will often produce school-based reasons for his inability to attend, simply because this is how he sees it. But while discussing his problem, he will soon admit that he does not in fact know why he cannot attend. There may be problems at school, and these must not be entirely discounted. But removal to another environment is not necessarily an answer. A boarding school may facilitate development by removing the child from the mother's influence, but this has not always proved effective. Furthermore, it also removes the child from local sources of treatment that might have been able to achieve something within the family context. Removal to special school or to hospital may provide a more permissive, and therefore therapeutic, environment in which the child may have a chance to work through his own problems. But even this makes treatment of the root causes difficult. It must however be agreed that in some instances only treatment of the child is possible. If it is considered that family therapy is impracticable then removing the child for treatment away from the family may be the best that circumstances will allow.

A further point that favours change after a period of absence is the child's difficulty in explaining his absence to his fellow pupils. He is ashamed of having been away without any apparent reason, and is afraid of being laughed at because it appears that he was afraid of coming to school. His anxiety is heightened by the fact that he has no comprehensible explanation for himself. Often it would seem that his fears on this account are imaginary and generated within himself because of his own lack of explanation. He derides himself far more than others deride him. Much of his basic difficulty lies in his assumption that his own self image is the image of him held by others. This enhances the value of the therapist's efforts to help him come to terms with his own problems and explain himself to himself.

However, if treatment is to aim at the proper development of the child and the establishment of mature relationships within the family, it will be in the context of the family that the most effective work will be done. While the child may receive psychotherapy at the expert hands of the psychiatrist, the latter will be kept constantly informed and brought up to date about family background and family relationships during the period of treatment. He will know from the work of everyone involved at what points in treatment it may be desirable to see one or both parents with or without the child. In this way the family is helped to become integrated and members to communicate with one another in a joint effort to solve their mutual problems and so meet the child's needs. Lack of communication results in fantasy and imaginings that increase the child's anxiety. The longer treatment is postponed the stronger becomes the influence upon the child of his own fantasy and this can only be allayed by helping him bring his fears into the open and test them against reality.

Treatment and the school

Attention has already been drawn to the need for a reasonable degree of flexibility in school management if the school refusing child is to be helped. Of course if the child is not at school there is nothing that his teachers can do. But the most important part the school can play is in early detection of school refusal. The reactions of infants to school attendance and separation from mother vary widely in the sorts of behaviour exhibited, and the time taken to "settle in." Any suggestion of excessive reaction or an over prolonged period of adaptation to the new life of school should receive careful attention and possibly referral. If later and more pronounced refusal is to be avoided the early symptoms should be investigated. If, by means of constant pressure, the infant is persuaded to suppress his symptoms these may well re-emerge at the end of the latency period because the relational difficulties have remained unresolved.

Nursery and infant schools offer immense opportunity for "family" education. The participation of parents in the life and activities of the school is becoming an increasing feature of these schools, and no opportunity should be missed of developing it and seeking ways whereby the staff and parents may communicate freely and be seen so to do by the children. This not only aids the difficult transition from home to school, but provides the observant teacher with the opportunity of detecting difficulties before they become problems and initiating treatment at a time when it prevents rather than cures.

In the later years of school, in junior and secondary education, both truancy and attendance difficulties of other sorts tend to receive less attention than is given them in the infant school. The main aim is to get the child back to school and ensure the continuance of his education which is seen as the school's primary task. It is assumed, rightly of course for the majority of children, that the older a child grows the more susceptible he should be to discipline and obedience to school rules. Since this is so, divergence from this pattern should always merit close attention. Not every case of truancy or absence without apparent cause is only a discipline problem. The trouble is that although most teachers would be prepared to give this attention, time and the overburdening of the services that are available for diagnosis and treatment often weigh heavily against them.

If school-phobia is associated, as most of the research seems to indicate, with malfunction of the child's normal relationships with others, then it is his interaction with his fellows or his expressed feelings towards them that will provide the material for treatment and will also be the indices of his condition. Although he may present physical symptoms of distress such as vomiting, stomach pains, headaches and so on, the treatment of these will not return him to normal functioning. Whatever therapeutic means of restoration are employed, whether at home, at school or in the clinic, they will need to discover how the child reacts to others, whether he is afraid of them, hates them, loves them or is afraid that they will not care about him or be friends with him. His image of himself stems from these feelings. It is because of them that he loses confidence and finds himself incapable of normal relationships. They must, therefore, be taken first. Children will often express their feelings and fears on paper, but treatment must extend beyond the release of pent-up emotions. This is a highly skilled activity and needs the expert handling of an experienced psychiatrist or medical practitioner. This is why proper treatment is so vital.

10

Where to Get Help

I. MEDICAL AND PSYCHIATRIC SERVICES

One of the problems which local and district government reorganization has been trying to tackle during the last few years is the multiplicity of services bearing upon the same family or individual. It was not uncommon, five or six years ago, to find a problem family being visited and possibly being treated by half a dozen different workers from as many social agencies, both statutory and voluntary. The result was confusion for the workers who were often unaware of each others' involvement or the line being taken in treatment or relief, and equal confusion for the family who either played one worker off against another or found that treatments tended to cancel each other out.

Recently many local authorities have been engaged in a mammoth reorganization of the educational, social and health services which they administer. The inspiration for reorganization has been the Seebohm Report. This made many recommendations for better and more efficient co-ordination of services, so that social workers should avoid over-specialization and broaden their services enabling one worker to treat more than one aspect of family need. But this change in the nature of the work has been resented by many groups of people who make use of the services offered. Educationalists are not always entirely happy to co-operate too closely with the social services, who have, they feel, different attitudes towards the children and the parents from those of the teachers and other persons involved in school management. Time, however, is likely to accustom the services to working together and using the best of each others' skills in the interests of their clients, and professional differences and reservations will diminish.

Whatever procedures may eventually emerge for inter-disciplinary co-operation, there are still a variety of different sources of help and guidance for the parent and child who are looking for ways of coping with the problems of truancy or refusal to attend school. As already mentioned, the first and perhaps most immediately obvious and accessible source of advice is the general practitioner. He is almost certainly known to one or both of the child's parents. Few parents have gone through the early years of child rearing without at some time or another making the professional acquaintance of their doctor. Many families have attended the same surgery on their own or their children's behalf for the whole of the children's lives. Doctors tend to be relatively permanent members of a community, and so may well have known since babyhood the child who is brought to them with a problem eight or ten years later. Whatever may be the results of National Health Service the family doctor is still one person who has individual status in the eyes of his patients which places him outside the system of education and social service. The added advantage of confidential consultation makes him approachable in situations where other workers are not approachable, at least not until a special relationship between worker and client has been established.

A parent who is deeply disturbed by his or her child's behaviour has many reservations about seeking outside help for the solution of the problem. The sense of guilt; protectiveness towards the child and a reluctance to recognize really disturbed behaviour. In such situations the doctor is a more approachable figure than some stranger who may be sent from the social services department, or someone associated with the school who may be felt to be prejudiced or already know too much about one side of the problem to be able to assess the parental side.

In describing those who consulted him on school-phobia problems Dr. Clyne, in his book *Absent: School Refusal as an Expression of Disturbed Family Relationships*, divides the parents into three groups. In most cases one parent, usually the mother, brings the child to the consulting room, father may appear later, but very seldom do both parents come together. The first group he describes are those mothers with a strongly protective attitude towards the child and a consequent reluctance to allow the child to be interviewed alone. Both child and mother revealed the inter-dependence which constituted a substantial element in the problem, but both child and mother also protected their independence by complaining of their dependence. The second group were marked by the evident sense of guilt which the mothers revealed. In such cases the mother alone would seek an interview, leaving the child in the waiting room. Explanations of the disturbance would aim at keeping deeper emotions hidden, but such parents had come for help in a situation they had been unable to resolve on their own and would be willing to hand over their child for treatment to someone else when they recognized their own failure.

With both these groups Dr. Clyne felt reasonably confident of being able to effect a reasonable cure by treatment. Though suppressing their fears and anxieties at first both groups were aware of their existence and had come because they sincerely wanted to unburden themselves and resolve the problem. But the third group presented more difficulty. These were parents who had come for assurance about the rightness of their method of dealing with the problem, and their right and good quality of mothering. These mothers regarded their children as being unbalanced through no fault of the parents. If they did not receive the assurance they wanted they were unlikely to come again, but if it was given they had little need of anything more except perhaps occasional reinforcement. The doctor's prognosis for such cases was doubtful, although the child might return to school his emotional disturbance remained undealt with and suppressed, and might well arise again at a later date.

Among the children interviewed by the doctor will be those with the specific somatic complaints already mentioned. These are fairly standardized "illnesses" in the sense that they are open to treatment by normal medical means. They may affect the stomach, throat or head and the doctor may take the normal course of treating them. But some children show no such complaints. Having achieved their main aim of staying away from school, their anxiety is alleviated and they have little to complain about. In such circumstances it is the mother who does the complaining as it is she who, with the child at home, is the chief sufferer.

In either case treatment has to be at a deeper level than what is superficially presented. To treat the "illness" at its face value may relieve the symptom, but it does not provide any real solution to the problem. In the second instance the child must eventually return to school, and this will only be achieved by tackling the problem at the deeper level of anxiety, and treating both parent and child according to their respective needs.

One advantage the doctor has over many other workers involved with the family is the deep rooted conception of a doctor as a confidant and one to whom a problem can be handed over. This image of the doctor exists in most patients, irrespective of the personality of the doctor. It is the general and justifiable image of the profession as a whole and is seen as part of the doctor's role. Other services have to earn such an image by their personal contact with the client. Mutual sympathy and involvement of doctor with patient and patient with doctor is very much eased by this conception of one another and the element of transference, in the psychoanalyst's sense of the term, becomes an essential element in the process of treatment. But, as Dr. Clyne points out, there are many ways of using the relationship between doctor and patient and great care must be exercised in the triangle of doctor-child-parent to avoid the alienation of one by the treatment of the other. The mother must not be made to feel that her child has been taken over or his affections alienated, similarly the child must not be allowed to feel that another parental figure has appeared on the scene, presenting the same degree of misunderstanding and hostility as may be found in the real parent. Some children may so identify with the doctor that they transfer their dependence from parent to doctor and so become just as difficult for the doctor to wean from dependence as the mother had found them.

For the general practitioner each case is a different case and generalizations will be dangerous. The essential need is for sensitivity to the needs of both child and parent so that an adequate diagnosis can be arrived at on which treatment can be based. Presenting symptoms must be distinguished from the deeper reasons which have caused a consultation to be sought. Another advantage enjoyed by the doctor is that each member of the family is equally his concern, and he has no professional constraints upon the exercise of his skills and insights. There is no other worker, except possibly the psychiatrist, who is similarly free from such constraints.

Although the general practitioner has such advantages in the treatment of children with emotional disorders, it must be remembered that not every G.P. has the inclination or interest to become involved in such treatment.

Like every other profession, doctors are very fully employed and compelled to limit their work to proportions which make it both effective and manageable. The treatment of such children can often be a time consuming occupation and it is understandable that many general practitioners feel that it is a job for the specialist or the educational service. There is the further difficulty that parents may need some persuasion to consult their doctor, especially if their child is not showing symptoms that can easily be described. The doctor may feel that he is being asked to deal with a vague problem which seems mainly a matter for the school and which would take time from his work for other patients who are making specific demands upon him.

These difficulties are very reasonable ones and the family doctor should be approached with some understanding of his position and the sort of information that will be helpful to him if he, in his turn, is to be helpful to the patient. He must decide if he wishes to treat the case or whether it is better transferred to the child guidance clinic. He will need to know the severity of the child's condition and match this to the probable delay if the case is referred to child guidance and the damage this delay may do. He must, very early in his diagnosis, determine who is to be treated, child or parent or both, together or singly. In this way he will have some idea of whether or not he has the time, inclination or ability to embark upon effective treatment.

The school medical officer

Since every local authority has a team of area or school medical officers it might well be asked why, as medical practitioners, they could not perform the same function in treatment as the general practitioners. In the first place they are school, and not family, doctors. In the second place, and more important for our purposes, they already have a very well defined function in relation to the school which occupies their working time fully. Finally, they are part of a total service which includes a psychiatric service based upon a clinic. They do however have a diagnostic role in cases referred to them. Such cases may be referred from any of the school services, teachers, educational welfare officers or educational psychologists. Such referrals are made when it would seem that professional guidance, beyond the competence of the particular service concerned, is needed. The medical officer may then decide whether or not to refer the matter for psychiatric treatment. Again, as with the general practitioner, there are administrative as well as medical factors to be considered. Since he is part of a team, with a foot in two camps—health and education—he will naturally look at the whole treatment service and determine where, within it, the child may best receive the attention that he needs. In making this assessment he will have in mind the local facilities for special educational treatment, as well as the child guidance service. He may refer the child to the latter for further expert opinion, or he may feel that adequate treatment is available elsewhere within the local authority services, including special schools, assessment centres and hospitals.

This, of course, raises the issue of reorganization of both health and social services, which is as yet in its infancy and about which, particularly in the health service, much has yet to be declared by the government and worked out at the local level. Some authorities have recently begun to authorize medical officers to assess children for admission to schools for the maladjusted. This authorization is the result of pressures upon the psychiatric services rather than the ideals of practice. But at least it may ensure more rapid treatment for a child, for if the psychiatrist has a long back-log of cases assessment might be delayed for two or three months, during which the child's condition could deteriorate with prolonged in-decision and absence from school.

The psychiatrist

The development of child guidance clinics illustrates the gradually expanding range of facilities available for the treatment of disturbed children, and the slow but steady process of integrating the professional skills that are needed for successful treatment. Although most local authorities in England and Wales run, or have access to, clinics with psychiatric and ancillary services, there is still a very considerable degree of understaffing, and not every clinic has the requisite professional staff. Staff are of course expensive, but it is unfortunate that because of some deep laid prejudice against psychiatric treatment children with bad teeth get a good professional service while those who have faulty emotional development which can cause as much pain and damage as any physical defect and cannot be artificially remedied, do not.

Ideally, every clinic should combine the professional skills of at least four persons—a psychiatrist, an educational psychologist, a psychiatric social worker and a remedial teacher and/or play therapist. With such a team both diagnosis and treatment are possible. It is necessary for information about a child to be obtained from both home and school. The educational psychologist is in constant close contact with the schools and teachers, he is also skilled in testing educational attainment and discovering learning difficulties and blockages. The social worker can obtain details about the child's home background and make arrangements for the attendance of parents at the clinic if this is necessary. He or she may also be able to undertake treatment in the home. With these sources of information and support the psychiatrist will be in a position to make his diagnosis of the children referred to him and carry out treatment, or recommend others to do so.

The position of the psychiatrist in the clinic is that of a director of a team. He is also the medical officer with responsibility for the patients referred to him. Assessment, diagnosis and treatment, whoever may separately be involved in them, are ultimately his responsibility. An approach to a psychiatrist in a clinic is therefore in all respects similar to the approach of the general practitioner, except for previous personal knowledge of the patient. He may, in fact, have more background through the work of his colleagues than would normally be available to the family doctor, unless the latter specifically asked for it.

The method of treatment used by the psychiatrist will differ from one patient to another according to age and background, but in most cases psychotherapy will be used in much the same way with each patient. It is important to establish an adequate relationship between doctor and patient within which the therapy can take place. This relationship will often duplicate or recapitulate unsatisfactory relationships in which the patient has been involved. But now this takes place in a controlled situation in which the therapist can resolve and bring to the surface fantasies and anxieties in such a way that the patient can cope with them, discarding the unreal and managing the real. Self-confidence may thus be gradually built up and independence achieved. This is an immense simplification of what is, in fact, a complex process which takes both time and effort. Therapy is not always successful, and the psychiatrist may have to accept partial success or even complete failure. Much depends upon what goes on between treatment sessions, how much backing is possible at home, how deep laid is the disturbance and how acceptable to the patient is the form of treatment.

Other members of the team may be called upon to assist in the treatment. Remedial teaching which helps the patient overcome a sense of failure by making progress

135

in any subject which causes anxiety in the school situation, can be a valuable part of the clinic's work. Play therapy is also a valuable means of both diagnosis and treatment. Children may be given figures and physical representations of the home or school situation. In free play with these the manner in which the child manipulates or places them can reveal much about his feelings towards other people in his environment and his relationship with them. Free or controlled play, according to the judgment of the therapist, can also aid the child's own disturbance in the same fashion as a normal child will work out his fantasies and anxieties with the toys at his disposal.

There will be situations when the psychiatrist decides to see the family unit as a whole, and to treat it in a unitary fashion. Although in the majority of cases the family case-work is delegated to the clinic social worker, recent insights into family group workings have suggested possibilities for group therapy. There is, however, the constant danger that the involvement of the therapist will result in a process of playing off one member against another in the effort to make objective assessments from a position of involvement within the group. There is also the possible danger of making, or appearing to make, the assumption that the child's disturbance has its roots solely within the dynamics of the family, whereas there may be many other contributory factors, either peculiar to the child or outside the group. These will necessitate individual work with the child against the background information provided by other team members.

In understanding the role of the psychiatrist it is essential to grasp his double professional associations. As local authority arrangements are at the time of writing, the child guidance clinic is the responsibility of the education department of the local authority. Both building and staff, with the exception usually of the psychiatric social worker who is appointed and paid by the health department, are paid for by the education committee. The psychiatrist is, however, a medical officer and is paid and appointed by the local hospital regional board and seconded by them to work with the education department. He thus has colleagues in both departments and is able to maintain a position of independence within each. From the point of view of his work he is in a good position for maintaining close relationships with the health service, including hospitals and consultant paediatricians, as well as the educationalists with whom he is working.

The next and necessary step in co-ordinating the services concerned with children with emotional disturbances is, as mentioned above, now in the process of being worked out between the education and the social service departments of the local authorities. As we shall see in the second part of this chapter, this is causing a certain amount of strain within both departments due partly to the differences of emphasis between the two departments over questions of treatment, and partly because of the demands being made by education for a service at least as full as the one to which they have been accustomed with their own officers.

In the whole process of diagnosis, from detection to treatment, there are critical points of referral which the present complexity of the service tends to complicate. A number of professionally skilled people are all involved in some way with the same child and, in general, with the same problem. In such a situation close co-ordination is essential if the child is first to be detected as disturbed, then to pass through the various processes of screening and reach treatment without being held up on the way by an inadequate diagnosis that did not take account of factors beyond the professional competence of one or other of the officers.

A final note must be added about the role of the family

doctor. I have discussed his position when a case comes directly to him, but when a case is under discussion in the school or with any of the clinic staff, it is essential that he should be brought in at the beginning of the case. He may only wish to be kept in touch with the clinic and be advised of the progress of treatment. He may wish to offer information or advice to the psychiatrist based upon his past knowledge and records of both child and family. He may wish to take an active part in the treatment itself. It is clearly important that any relevant part of the past medical history of the family should be available to the psychiatrist, especially if drugs are administered to the child in the course of treatment. Equally, the family doctor should know of any treatment received by his patients which he himself did not prescribe.

2.   SOCIAL AND EDUCATIONAL SERVICES

The child guidance clinic

Apart from the psychiatrist the member of clinic staff who plays a substantial part in treatment is the psychiatric social worker. The P.S.W. is close to the psychiatrist, since it is to him that he or she is principally reporting in order to provide a constant supply of information about the child's background. She is a field officer in that the bulk of work will be done in the homes and schools of the children, rather than in the clinic. She will return to the clinic to complete reports and case histories from which other members of the team will get the information that they need.

The crucial work is therefore the interviewing, not only the parents of the child, but other persons who make up the child's environment at school as well as at home. In this way the social worker becomes familiar with the schools which are attended by children with whom she is likely to be dealing. She gets to know head teachers and will be able to discuss with them points which are not developed in formal reports. She will know the officers who may already have had contact with the child or the family, particularly the education welfare officers and educational psychologists. Although co-ordination with the social service department of the local authority may not yet be fully operative, the very nature of the work and the common basis of training and interest will almost certainly ensure co-operation between the two agencies.

The importance of field work cannot be over estimated. It is the only way in which it is possible to ensure that treatment for the child takes account of the whole of the child's personality and experience. Emotional disturbance of any kind is very complex in its origins and causes, unlike a physical illness it cannot be treated in isolation from the other pressures and relationships which are important parts of the child's life. Explanations of a child's behaviour can only be found if the various parts of the jig-saw of home, school and neighbourhood are fitted together to make a coherent picture. Only a skilled observer and interviewer can do this job of fitting one part into another. Once a picture begins to emerge treatment on a co-ordinated plan becomes possible. The psychiatrist will determine what sort of treatment is required and will, himself, deal directly with the child. But the social worker by knowledge and experience in family case-work, will supplement the clinical treatment, by indirect treatment. This will involve careful and often long term work with the family.

From all that has already been said about the connection between school-phobia and the dynamics of the family group, it is clear that the purpose of case-work with the family must be the relieving of suppressed or not readily admitted feelings of frustration, inadequacy or guilt; parents desperately want explanations of a situation which causes them deep distress and which they cannot handle themselves. The purpose of the case-work with the parents will, in the first instance, be to help them towards tentative explanations, not necessarily definitive ones, as these are seldom really possible; but by friendly and close relationships with the whole family, to bring into the open the complicated way in which many factors bear upon the child's behaviour, and how these factors are frequently ones for which no guilt need be felt and may, indeed, lie in the childhood experiences of the parents themselves for which they were in no way responsible. As understanding comes by patient discussion so, one by one, aggravating circumstances can be brought forward and ways of dealing with them examined. In some cases these circumstances may be beyond correction or alteration and the pressures on the child cannot be relieved, in such cases the removal of the child from the situation may have to be considered. This can be distressing or it may be welcomed by both child and parents. Whichever way it goes it will require proper thought and preparation. If the child is to attend a school some way from home, preliminary visits and interviews can be arranged. Parental involvement will ensure that the child does not feel rejected and the move is seen by all as a new start and a time for re-assessment of relationships on a new footing. The knowledge that the social worker already has of the appropriate schools will facilitate this move and ensure, as far as the available provision makes possible, the choice of the right school and the co-operation of the head teacher in the sort of treatment that the child needs. The following case history illustrates the procedure and content of the social worker's engagement with the family of a child referred for school-phobia.

The referral of Paul, aged fourteen, to the child guidance clinic came from the educational welfare officer via the school and area medical officers of health, and the letter requesting an interview for him was passed to the social worker who consulted the psychiatrist to arrange an interview. Unfortunately there had to be some delay owing to pressure of work and the interview could not take place for a fortnight. This made it all the more important for the family to have the support of the social worker for the intervening period.

A letter was sent immediately to the parents, giving the date of the interview for Paul and saying that a call would be made by the clinic social worker immediately. The first interview was tentative and exploratory, an easy and informal relationship was established with the mother, and Paul was seen for a short chat.

Both the school and the E.W.O. were interviewed and gave what information they could about Paul, and the clinic secretary contacted the family doctor. Because of the waiting period, the social worker saw Paul four times and could present a reasonably full report to the psychiatrist. Since the school reported that Paul had no special learning difficulties and regarded him as of good general intelligence and ability it was felt unnecessary to get a report from the educational psychologist. The social worker's report began with the family structure. Both parents are in their late forties and both worked, mother part-time. Paul is the seventh of eight children of whom only the last three are now at home, an elder sister of sixteen and a younger brother of thirteen. Father has always been a rather inadequate character and has been in trouble for drinking. He was interested in the children when they were young, but lost interest as they became independent and critical of his drinking. There is no real relationship between father and the children. The paternal grandparents live in Scotland and there is no contact with the family.

Mother has a background of inadequate upbringing, first by her grandmother and then by a great-aunt. She has no close relations. She has suffered from asthma since she was an adolescent. There has been some marital friction in the past, mostly caused by father's drinking and mother has left home on three occasions taking the children with her. The last occasion was four years ago. Although now living together, it is not on anything approaching a satisfactory basis and father is away from home for long periods. The living conditions of the family are sparse and untidy, and the flat offers inadequate accommodation for three adolescent children.

The report then turned to Paul. He presented most of the characteristics that have become associated with school-phobia. His mother told the social worker quite readily the symptoms he had shown. After doing his paper round he would come home complaining of headache and stomach pains. He would cry and accuse his mother of not believing him and not caring. Under pressure he would get as far as the bus but not be able to get on. He would wander off and go to see his married sister who lived ten miles away. He would sometimes hitch-hike farther than this. On returning home he would shut himself in his room and read. He was frequently tired and depressed, would sleep during the day, and watch television. He would go out walking during the night and eat very inadequately.

The family doctor's report showed a normal child until the last year, when sleeping problems arose. He was put on sleeping tablets for a short period but these resulted in difficulty in waking him in the mornings. His relationship with his mother had always been affectionate and clinging, as a young child he would get very anxious when she went out. He gets along all right with other boys but is embarrassed by the company of girls (according to mother.)

The psychiatrist interviewed Paul, and after consultation with the social worker decided that the best course was to place him in a school for maladjusted children where he would be away from the home and would not have to face the continual anxiety of getting to school. The social worker told Paul and his mother about this decision which both accepted quite readily. Since the selected school had a social worker on the staff the clinic worker withdrew from the case and the file was closed.

This case illustrates a relatively straightforward method of procedure in what was an easily diagnosed case. Had there been no social worker attached to the school the clinic worker would have continued contact as long as was felt desirable. The psychiatrist himself however visits the school weekly so that cases have a follow through from the clinic. This is obviously a very advantageous practice and of great value to both school and child.

The school psychological service and the clinical psychologist

The Education Act of 1944 laid upon local education authorities the duty of assessing the abilities and aptitudes of children, so that throughout their school career children might have the most suitable form of educational treatment available to them. The service is a school-based one, and responsibility is to the chief education officer. In addition to the school psychological service it is customary for the child guidance clinic to have an educational psychologist as part of its team, although he or she will be more aptly described as a clinical psychologist as the work will take place in the clinical setting.

In the school the psychologist will be concerned particularly with children referred to him by the head teacher for some learning difficulty, such as general backwardness or backwardness in a basic subject such as reading. Backwardness is of various sorts with varying causes, among which are emotional disturbances originating in the home or in the child's past development. A further impediment to learning is often found in behaviour problems with which teachers find it difficult to deal. Truancy and school-phobia are among such problems.

The psychologist will also be concerned with groups of children who have common learning difficulties and need the help of a remedial teacher. The inclusion of children in such a group may often be the result of tests administered by the school psychologist to ascertain reading or number standards and general intelligence. The psychologist is often asked to address groups of parents or teachers in order to deepen their understanding of child development or help them in dealing with the different emotional problems that are a normal result of the growth of the child's personality.

An essential feature of the training of a psychologist is how to test children in various ways so that a quantifiable estimate of their abilities or aptitudes may be reached as objectively as possible. For this reason a psychologist may often seem to be more objectively accurate in his assessments than the psychiatrist. But the complementary nature of each has to be understood, as well as the vaguer areas of overlap that inevitably occur. Since learning problems are closely related to emotional states the psychologist will frequently be concerned with tests that inquire into the emotional conditions of the child and the various factors that condition this, which often relate to home events and relationships. This is most likely to be so when it is a behaviour problem that is under discussion. The school may feel that it should be competent to deal with this and with a little help from the psychologist everything can be cleared up quite satisfactorily. The parents, too, will want to be persuaded that there is nothing seriously amiss and that their child can be back to normal without making a "thing" of it all. The mere mention of the word "psychiatrist" too often causes parents serious misgivings about their child's sanity. It is in this situation of professional boundary disputes that the psychologist will benefit from a team approach to the child's problem which will bring in the skills and knowledge of all the different professional expertise that is available. There is always a possibility of problems being disposed of in the easiest way because those concerned do not want to admit that the problem exists; it is up to the psychologist to ensure that referral to the clinic is not delayed nor bypassed by what may appear to be more acceptable treatment methods.

The therapeutic side of the psychologist's work should not be obscured. Although mainly concerned with assessment he will also, through remedial work with individual children, restore confidence by bringing them back to a normal learning situation. He will also have a therapeutic role for the teacher whose professional confidence in his ability to cope with a learning problem may be shaken by his failure with an individual child. The psychologist is an educational colleague and his advice and help with the child, especially in school refusal and truancy, will reinforce the sense of professional competence against the attack that appears to be made upon it by the child, and possibly the parents also.

The education welfare officer

The first person to take action outside the boundaries of the school in cases of non-attendance, is the school welfare officer. He is usually based upon one of the schools in the area that he serves, but will visit other schools on a regular basis or upon request. Cases of persistent non-attendance for which no medical reason is given will be brought to his notice by the head teacher, or he may himself examine the registers and make enquiries about a particular child's atendance record which he regards as unsatisfactory. In the early stages of the service he was regarded as simply an attendance officer whose function was to bring about the speedy return of children to school, principally by applying or threatening to apply the law of compulsory school attendance. But as the service has grown his role has broadened and the number of cases actually brought to the juvenile court has diminished.

In addition to enforcing attendance he has also become concerned with the wide range of services to which children and parents are entitled, such as free meals, school clothing, assistance with transport costs and so on. His work has always been heaviest in areas in which social deprivation is most severe and the economic circumstances of the parents have demanded application for many of the helping facilities that are available to them. This side of his work has, of course, led to close contact with the social service departments which may be working with the same families as himself.

Recruitment to the education welfare service has, to the very considerable advantage of the service, been very largely from people with experience of contact with the general public and knowledge of the ordinary affairs of family life. Specialization has been avoided, as the main requirement of the work, apart from a knowledge of educational administration, is the ability to recognize the problems that may affect families with young children and a sympathetic approach towards helping them through them. This demands a thorough acquaintance with local provision for children's needs. It also requires an ability to recognize problems for what they are and not generalize about absence in such a way as to assume that all non-attendance is due to one cause or that blame always lies in one place. The emotional side of the problem must receive as much attention as the social.

The general principle under which the welfare officer must work is return of the child to school. But in his efforts to achieve this he works to some extent as a social worker might, helping both child and parent to recognize the force of law not just as "them and us," but as a social principle which is to their advantage. In this form of dialogue he will recognize very quickly the limits imposed by his own terms of reference, and resort to referral through the school medical officer as soon as he is aware of the need for specialized treatment.

Some educational authorities have recognized the need for early referral and detection of emotional disturbances in children, and steps have been taken to shift the emphasis of the welfare officer's work towards detection of difficulties and the securing of specialized treatment as soon as possible. The Children and Young Persons Act of 1969 stressed the necessity for early recognition and assessment of children's needs and for a variety of forms of treatment to be available. These provisions are proving valuable in the treatment of truancy when this is associated with home conditions that suggest a need for care and control by the courts. The Local Authority Social Services Act of 1970 leaves much to the individual local authority as to how it co-ordinates its welfare services, but it gives the opportunity for a much closer system of co-operation in family welfare services than has hitherto been possible.

Welfare officers themselves are in two minds about transfer to social service departments, because of the additional demands likely to be made upon them in their new role. At present they are able to give the schools a good service, but if further tasks are laid upon them as part of an overall family service the educational side of the work is likely to suffer. The problem, as always, is one of staff shortages and pressure of work.

School counselling

The school counselling service is still a relatively young one, having begun as recently as 1965. Counsellors as specialized members of staff in secondary schools are still the exception rather than the rule, and pastoral care within large schools is mainly the responsibility of individual memebrs of staff. Where counsellors do exist, however, their function is very much part of the general welfare service. Working within the school, and constantly available to the pupils, they acquire a knowledge of the many different problems that youngsters present. These include relationships with parents as well as anxieties about affairs in school itself. Their presence in a school increases the chances of early detection of emotional disturbance, but their main concern remains with the problems of "normal" children, and much time must necessarily be given to vocational guidance and the personal problems which affect the school leaver.

In addition to the school counselling service other experiments are suggested or being carried out to improve the educational/social services which can be offered to schools and parents. The teacher/social worker has been suggested for schools in areas of special need, to deal with such problems as truancy and delinquency. This type of worker is now a practical reality due to the development of social service departments which are providing a service to schools. One authority is currently planning for the appointment of liaison workers who, though not necessarily fully qualified social workers, would be specially trained to work in the general area of school welfare. They would meet head teachers and other members of staff in both primary and secondary schools on a regular weekly basis. They would be based upon the appropriate area social services office, where they would be in immediate contact with senior social workers with whom they could discuss referrals and the advisability of passing any of these on to specialized staff for treatment. Under such a scheme the co-ordination of educational welfare and social services would be assured. This scheme also provides for an adequate school service from workers specifically designated for it, who would not be involved in other social work activities which would detract from their school responsibility.

School attendance and the law

Education is compulsory for all children of school age and responsibility for seeing that they are properly educated rests with the parents. It is, of course, education which is compulsory not attendance at school, but once a child is registered as attending school, absence from school is assumed to be absence from education and hence is a breach of the law, unless a good cause, such as illness, is the reason. Some children are, for valid reasons, educated in their own homes or in hospital, but in such cases they are registered by the local authority as receiving education according to age and ability and the law is observed.

In cases of truancy and school-phobia the local authority, through its welfare services, may bring a court order against the parents of the child. This is known as a School Attendance Order and a fine may be imposed upon the parents. If a child suffering from school-phobia is attending a clinic for treatment he would of course be absent for medical reasons, and no proceedings would be taken. Truancy, however, presents greater difficulties.

As already noted, the dividing line between truancy and school-phobia is not easy to define. It is now recognized as having, in the words of the Seebohm Report, "deeper roots and wider implications than the symptom of persistent non-attendance." It is also recognized as being a malaise of poor social and environmental conditions which are not always ones from which parents can easily escape. On the other hand, the courts know that there is a close association between truancy and subsequent delinquent behaviour. It is necessary, therefore, to decide first about the desirability of treatment if such is available, recognizing the possibility of the child being emotionally disturbed and a case of school-phobia rather than truancy. The court may, however, decide that the truancy is wilful on the part of the child, or the result of irresponsibility on the part of the parents. In such cases probation may be the best decision, and the probation officer given the task of securing the child's attendance. In view of the association of truancy with delinquency the intervention of the probation service at an early stage is a wise precaution. These are the officers most likely to be aware of the problems involved, and who will know the associates of the truant child and the dangers which he may face.

Children brought to the court may be committed to the care of the local authority. This would make available the services of the local assessment centre, where children may be placed under the observation of specialists for a brief period with the purpose of deciding upon the best sort of treatment for them. It also enables the child to have a period away from home which is often a valuable break in a possibly difficult or stressful situation for both child and parents. When home circumstances have militated against the child's normal development, substantial changes are often observable during a period away from home. While at the assessment centre children may receive education on the premises, and remedial teachers are available to deal with specific problems. This gives the court the opportunity to receive further reports upon the child and hence to recommend appropriate treatment.

Whatever the decision of the court, the involvement of the social and probation services will ensure that some action is possible at the source of the problem, namely the family. The number of cases brought to court will decrease as the services available become more closely co-ordinated and treatment facilities increase. The real need is for such a degree of flexibility and co-ordination that both detection and treatment can be speedy and offered without undue administrative delay. This demands that schools, social services and education departments make every possible effort to establish good relationships between themselves and the community they serve. Much can be achieved if the community itself is aware of the services available and is accustomed to making use of them. The idea that calling in the help of welfare or social workers is somehow a slur upon parental capabilities must be dispelled.

Conclusion

SCHOOL-PHOBIA and truancy are still ill-defined terms in spite of the efforts of research workers to separate clearly the characteristics of each. The trouble lies not so much with the difficulty of definition as with the procedure of assessment as the definitions come to be applied to individual children. Each child with an attendance problem needs careful investigation before any really reliable conclusion can be reached about the real nature of his disturbance. Such investigation is time consuming and requires the participation of experts. This is where the severest difficulties lie, since the expertise required is expensive and in short supply. This means that considerable responsibility must continue to rest with the schools and the staff who have the first and best opportunity for early detection of children suffering from emotional disturbance. If such detection can be effected early, and recent proposals for the increase of school-based welfare services implemented, then the disadvantages of shortage may be at least partially overcome.

Writing in 1966, Margery Cooper summarized research on truancy and school-phobia and concluded that some modification in school attitudes and organization could very effectively improve the chances of children. The critical points in a child's school career could be examined for opportunities of lessening the pressures to which children are subjected. Change of school is one such period at which stress is suffered. At the early stages of entry, and at the point of transfer from infant to junior school

153

staggered entry and half-day attendance are the kinds of variations that could give teachers a better opportunity than they have at present to give time and attention to the individual child. In the junior school reduction of competitive experiences would reduce pressures which contribute to disturbed behaviour. Whatever is done to relieve tension through reorganization or modification of curriculum must be accompanied by increased emphasis in teacher training upon the recognition and treatment of young children's problems. Much depends upon the personalities of teachers and research into procedures of selection on the basis of personality could improve the methods of recruitment of teachers.

The need for more research has already been stressed. Too little is known to make really valid assertions about truancy and school-phobia and the various modes of treatment and their effectiveness on a nation-wide basis. The relationship between school administration and teaching methods and the general incidence of school refusal has received minimal attention.

In a later article in which Margery Cooper drew together the facts accumulated about school-phobia and truancy she concluded, in spite of the suggestions that had been made about possible action at the school level, that "the role of the school in school refusal appeared to be a minimal one." This may suggest that the school can do little to offset the effects of refusal, but this would be to underestimate the possibilities of "treatment" at the school level. As things are at present it would seem that any marked increase in the treatment services available is a long way away. We have made it clear in the preceding chapters that the root causes of refusal lie in relationships at home, but this does not preclude the active role of the teacher in detecting and assisting the child in the same way as teachers in many areas are able to detect and offset many of the bad effects of environmental deprivation.

The relationship of home and school is still less than adequate in areas where education is undervalued, it is also frequently inadequate when the child's problems are such as to incur a sense of guilt or inadequacy in the parents themselves. I sincerely hope that what little information has been offered here may help to bring parents and teachers closer together in a mutual effort to solve the problems of the children who are the subject of intense concern to both.

Books for Further Reading

THE following books each contain full lists of titles and articles for further reading, and very adequately cover the research so far carried out in Great Britain and the U.S.A.

Clyne, Max B., *Absent* (Tavistock Publications, 1966)

Kahn, J. H. & Nursten, J. P., *Unwillingly to School* (Pergamon Press, 1964)

Tyerman, M. J., *Truancy* (University of London Press, 1968)

Other books bearing upon the subjects discussed:

Hargreaves, D. H., *Interpersonal relations and education* (Routledge & Kegan Paul, 1972)

Rutter, M., *Maternal Deprivation* (Penguin Books, 1972)

Schaffer, H. R., *The growth of Sociability* (Penguin Books, 1971)

Stott, D. H., *Saving children from Delinquency* (U.L.P.)

Stott, D. H., *Unsettled children and their families* (U.L.P., 1959)

Winnicott, D. W., *The Child the Family and the Outside World* (Penguin Books)

Winnicott, D. W., *The Maturational Process and the Facilitating Environment* (Hogarth Press, 1965)

Younghusband, E. (ed.), *Social Work with Families* (Allen & Unwin, 1965)

Young, M. & McGeeney, P., *Learning Begins at Home* (Routledge & Kegan Paul, 1968)

Index